FLY FISHING
FOR SALMON

Out to the Backing, by W. B. Barrington-Browne.

FLY FISHING FOR SALMON

Edited by
JACK CHANCE

ADAM AND CHARLES BLACK
LONDON

First published 1973
A. & C. BLACK LTD
4, 5 & 6 Soho Square
London W1V 6AD

ISBN 0 7136 1374 2

By the special wish of the owner of the manuscript the author's royalties will be given to The Atlantic Salmon Research Trust.

Printed in Great Britain
by W & J Mackay Limited, Chatham

Contents

Drawings

Introduction

The author of this book wrote it while under treatment in hospital for an illness which was to prove fatal. It arose from notes he had made for a talk on fly fishing for salmon, which he had given to the boys of a preparatory school, and which he had illustrated with blackboard diagrams, and with examples of the equipment required for the sport.

The talk created enthusiasm amongst the boys, and led to a request by a number of the author's friends for his notes to be expanded into what he modestly defined as a "pamphlet", with no expectation of publication.

Shortly before his death the author gave the manuscript to the lady who is now my wife as a token of their long friendship. When she asked me to read it my first thought was that this would be one more in an endless chain of books on fishing from which, as a reviewer, I had concluded that too many were already in print.

Long before I had reached the end I had made up my mind that this was certainly not a book only for those who, as beginners, wished to acquire the basic essentials of fly fishing for salmon. There was much information and valuable advice in it which would, I felt sure, be of benefit to anglers like myself who have fished on salmon rivers for several decades and who, as in my case, have over the years ignored or forgotten some of the maxims impressed upon us by our parents or by those kind friends from whom we received our first lessons.

My wife does not claim to be an experienced fly fisher, although she has killed salmon and trout. But she gladly consented to publication, provided that the author's royalties should benefit some appropriate cause.

Aylmer Tryon (The Tryon Gallery Ltd) and the artist, Bill Barrington-Browne, have kindly allowed the use of the painting shown on the jacket.

There are, of course, and always have been, a multitude of deserving causes, but we could think of none more appropriate to the theme and none which would have appealed more whole-heartedly to the author than The Atlantic Salmon Research Trust, which did not exist at the time of his death. This Trust, set up a few years ago under the auspices of The Fishmongers Company and the Salmon and Trout Association, has as its main objective nothing more nor less than the conservation of the species in a world rapidly becoming despoiled by increasing populations, and by the evils which inevitably follow—pollution, excessive water extraction, high seas netting, and by the consequential constriction of salmon habitat in both sea and fresh water.

The Trust is seeking to achieve its aims in a variety of ways, by sponsoring research into the habits and life cycle of the Atlantic salmon on an international basis, and by acting as a focal point for the reception and dissemination of factual information obtained from many of the nations which either produce or benefit from the capture, sale or consumption of salmon.

As editor, I have preserved the text as it stands, with only minimal changes here and there to bring the work into the realm of current thought and practice. Where I have disagreed with the author, or have felt that additional data was needed, I have added a footnote to explain why.

JACK CHANCE
Past-President of
The Flyfishers' Club

Author's Note

A great many excellent books have been written on salmon fishing but they nearly all, as far as I know, try to cover the whole field and in most cases are altogether over the head of the non-expert. The novice should not attempt too much to start with—he should merely learn the rudiments: he should learn to cast and present the fly, but the complicated methods of casting, such as—the Spey cast, the Switch cast etc. can come later on, when he is quite happy with a rod. He can also postpone learning greased line fishing, which is a demanding art and which can be very successful under certain conditions, at a later date.

He should, of course, learn how to *hook* a fish and how to *play* him and *land* him. He must of course study the water and try to learn where to fish and there are quite a number of DON'TS that he should know.

That is all that is attempted in this short book.

From a book you cannot learn the whole art of salmon fishing but you can learn to avoid many disastrous mistakes and you can learn endless wrinkles which will make your fishing more finished and much more effective. It is also essential to know what to buy and what not to buy. This will save you a lot of expense.

If, after reading this book, you wish to pursue the matter further and have the ambition to become a good fisherman, then do not rely on books—practice and the example of an expert are the only things which will make you one. But even if you cannot achieve this goal you will still derive the utmost pleasure from trying.

I am deeply indebted to one or two friends of the experienced class who have been kind enough to read the typescript and make comments and valuable additions.

It is mainly written for the benefit of non-expert and holidays only fishermen, in the hopes that they will not be led astray by bad advice.

Here, once again, I would like to point out that I am not so conceited as to think that my opinions on this very controversial subject are always right. All I am trying to do is to pass on the experience of one who has given a great deal of thought to the matter for a great number of years and has taken the advice of many very experienced fishermen.

[1]

Origin and habits of the Atlantic Salmon

In the first place he should learn something about the salmon and his origin and habits, the salmon being the king of all fresh water fish.

As to the life-history of the salmon, our knowledge of it, thanks to scale reading, the systematic marking of fish and to limited research on both sides of the Atlantic ocean, is only just now beginning to be of any worth.

SPAWNING

This takes place roughly from October to January. Spawning is accomplished in the following manner. The male and female fish select a suitable place in the running water where the bed is gravel of the right size and consistency and play around it for some time. They then begin to make a furrow by working up the gravel with their noses and tails. When the furrow is made they throw themselves on their sides and rubbing against each other the hen fish ejects her ova into it and the male (or cock) fertilises them by covering them with milt. They cover the furrow with loose gravel and proceed upstream. Although the roe of the female contains from 17,000 to 20,000 eggs, only one egg can be exuded at a time. The fish, therefore, continue increasing the number of furrows for several days and form a bed or redd about twelve feet by eight or ten. The spawning bed is easily recognised by the thrown-up gravel; by some it is said to resemble an onion bed. The male fish keeps guard and chases off intruders, which may include small parr which are sexually mature and able to fertilise the eggs. Some say that the male salmon does not help in any way to dig the redd. Should the male fish be destroyed in the act of spawning, the female leaves the bed and retires to some deep pool to find another mate. The ova remain in these beds completely covered with loose gravel for several weeks or till the more genial warmth of spring allows hatching—Mergansers are a great peril to the ova at this stage. From the gravel the young fish emerge, their tails appearing first. These spawning redds are situated usually in the upper reaches of the river particularly in side or feeder streams and burns. The hen takes from 3 to 10 days to complete spawning. The fry emerge after 3 to 4 months. These little fish about 1in. long are called parr. After one year they are about 4in. long. Salmon parr suffer the most appalling depredation at the hands of gulls, heron, pike and cannibal trout, cormorants, mergansers, floods, falls and rapids, and their numbers are greatly diminished by the time that they acquire their silver coats and become smolts at 2 years. Sketches of main predators are shown in fig. 1. Smolts increase very rapidly in weight at this stage. They usually go down to the sea in May and return to the river either (1) the following year about July and August as grilse (3 years) when they weigh anything between 4 and 6lb. (grilse can easily be distinguished from salmon because they have a forked tail whereas the mature salmon's tail is straight) or (2) they remain in the sea another 6 to 8 months and come up the river for the first time in the spring of next year as salmon (4 years); at this stage they weigh anything from 7 to 10lb, or more. If they do come up as grilse they usually spawn early and return to the sea as kelts after a few months in the river. . . . Both these fish (whether grilse or salmon) usually remain at sea for 2 years and then return to the river for the second time as salmon (6 years); their weight at this stage depends entirely as to where they have been feeding in the sea, they may be anything from 9 to 18lb or more.

An interesting point about a salmon is his teeth. A fresh salmon straight up from the sea with sea lice on him has razor sharp teeth. After a few days his teeth get blunter and loose like a baby's first teeth. After 15 days he has lost all his teeth. After spawning a kelt forms new teeth.

Otter

Merganser

Cormorant

THE
ENEMIES

Heron

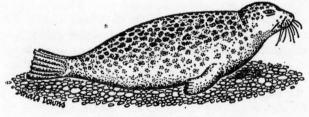

Seal.

1. The main predators of the salmon.

Another feature about salmon is that they will always try to return to the same river and to the same spawning grounds. No one knows yet where salmon go at sea for their feeding grounds but it is obvious that some of these feeding grounds must be very much better than others.*

For instance the Beauly fish average 8 to 10lb, whereas those in the Welsh Dee average about 15 to 16lb. Salmon fry need more oxygen to enable them to survive than is contained in salt water and there is more oxygen in the fast running head-waters of our rivers than in the deep sluggish pools—this explains the urge of the salmon to ascend the seemingly impossible shallow waters in tiny burns to make their spawning beds.

Another interesting thing about salmon is that they always run in to a river on a high tide (see page 70 "Tides"). It is the uncontrollable urge to spawn that drives them back to their river—always to the same river when possible and always to the same spawning grounds; but they again have to run the gauntlet of countless dangers before they reach their goal; such as drift nets out at sea—these are sometimes 100ft deep and 500yds long and made of nylon—seals at the river mouth and nets in the estuary, and again, in some cases, nets higher up the river, and then all the way up the river they not only have to negotiate rapids, falls and weirs and floods, but also all the fishermen and in some rivers poachers and otters. They can travel 25 to 35 miles per day. If they are very lucky they may succeed in reaching their spawning grounds. The consensus of opinion is that salmon do not feed in fresh water. This is such a controversial subject and such a lot has

* *Editorial note:* Unhappily, some of the feeding grounds have been discovered by netsmen in the high seas, particularly in the Davis Strait off the west coast of Greenland. From this area by inshore netting, drift-netting and by "long line" with hooks baited with sandworms, thousands of metric tons of salmon, many immature, have been removed within the last ten years. Under pressure from the Atlantic salmon producing countries, particularly Canada, U.S.A. and Great Britain, the Danish Government has now passed legislation for a phased cessation of high seas netting for salmon off West Greenland over the years 1973–5, and thereafter for a total ban on this fishing from 1 January, 1976. Fishing by Greenlanders inside Greenland's territorial limits will continue, however, but will be limited to a maximum catch of 1100 metric tons annually.

been written about it that I do not propose to go into it at any length here—sufficient to say, I do not think salmon FEED in fresh water in the sense that they wish to EAT—(except kelts on their way down to the sea—kelts will be dealt with later). Possibly a salmon takes a fly or bait as an instinctive reaction to something which resembles his food in the sea. I am sure it is more out of *curiosity* or *anger* that a salmon takes a fly or a bait—very seldom is anything ever found in the stomach, though there have been cases of this. It looks to me as if he takes the fly or bait into his mouth to CHEW it in order to extract the juice, which he thinks is there and then SPITS it out; it is at this point we must HOOK him before he succeeds in doing so. We will deal with that later* (see pages 59-63).

KELTS

A kelt is a spent salmon, that is to say a salmon which has spawned.

I will try to give you some idea of how to tell a clean spring fish from a really well-mended kelt. It is a question that has caused agonies of doubt to the inexperienced fisher, or to the fisher who has had but little spring fishing, because if he brings home the wrong fish, besides breaking the law—which probably won't trouble him so much—he will incur the merciless chaff of his friends. In the first place let me warn you that silvery brightness is no proof of the fish being a clean fish. On the contrary, a clean fish, though very brilliant, is not such a dead white as a kelt. In the water the clean fish flashes rather a golden colour, the kelt a dead or silvery white. But if, when a fish is landed, a rosy pink flush—a

---

* *Editorial note:* Another theory, which I find more convincing and for which I do not claim the origin, is based on the thesis that a salmon's behaviour in fresh water is governed by the paramount desire to mate and reproduce. The fish, therefore becomes intensely suspicious of any strange surface or sunk object which floats or swims into its purview. If the object be classed as an intruder and therefore a possible menace to survival it has to be attacked and destroyed. This theory does not, however, explain the fact that for long periods salmon remain inactive and ignore the most compelling lure. It cannot therefore be the only motive for siezing fly or bait. One thing is certain—the argument will persist for as long as salmon continue to ascend rivers, just as it has since rod fishing for them began some centuries ago, and we may feel grateful that this is so.

peach-coloured opalescence—can be plainly seen along the belly and sides, that fish is a clean fish. Then that fish will be such a good fish that there can be no room for doubt.

He will be short and thick "as hard as a board". The real difficulty arises with spring fish that have been a long time up from the sea and have lost something of their condition; even then they are shapely fish, and that, after all, is the very best test of the question clean or kelt. Thickness is the one thing that the kelt never has. If a fish looks long and lean, put him back; he is a kelt, however bright he may be and however clean his gills. But if the gills of a lean fish are infested with that maggot-like parasite, then that makes his keltship undeniable; the great majority of kelts have this horrible parasite devouring the fringes of their gills, or else show the whitish lumps and scars where they have been at work. But the presence of this parasite is not absolute proof that the fish on which they are found is a kelt. I have seen one or two, though rarely, on the gills of undoubted and unquestionable fresh fish.

A slack vent also indicates that the owner is a kelt; the vent of a clean-run fish is hard and firm and will not protrude, as does the kelt's, if the stomach nearby is pressed in.

A really good fresh-run spring fish will generally have all the fins clean and hard, and will show no sore or redness on the lower ray of the tail. A kelt, on the other hand, will generally (but not always) show a frayed and raw tail, and some signs of scraping and redness along the whole under side of the fish. This redness and fraying is a bad sign, but not necessarily fatal. A spring fish that has lain in the river for some time will often show some redness of the lower ray of the tail fin, and may show other abrasions and redness along the belly.

Of the points I have mentioned no one item is decisive, but the accumulation of several almost always makes it fairly clear what your verdict ought to be upon the question "kelt or clean".

The signs of the kelt are:
1. Gill maggots.
2. Leanness, or rather a want of plumpness and an apparently large head.
3. A slack and easily protruded vent.

4. Frayed tail and fins.
5. A fishy smell, and scales coming off easily.

The characteristics of a spring fish are:

1. Shapely form, in particular, depth from back to belly.
2. No fishy smell.
3. Clean gills.
4. A hard, firmly closed vent.
5. Generally dark fins, not abraded, or very little abraded by lying on the river bottom.

The flesh also is harder and firmer than that of the kelt, but this point is more easily noticed after death, and you must make up your mind promptly whilst the question of life or death hangs in the balance. And when you decide that the fish is a kelt you must return him or her to the water as soon as possible, provided you have got the hook out instantly and without holding him down. If you have played him for long, or have had to hold him down firmly to get out the hook from his jaws, the fish will be much exhausted, and if you fling him in carelessly he will very probably turn over on his back and die. You must slip him gently into the water, and if he does not quickly swim off you must prop him upright in the shallows between two stones in a current and with his head upstream, and there he will slowly recover his strength. But if a kelt has been much exhausted you will often find him still lying there like a log a quarter or even half an hour after you have left him. Then it is as well not to leave him so, or he may be attacked by foxes, otters, or herons. If you walk up to him he will probably bolt off into deep water and will be safe.

A salmon has frequently got a great many black spots (or X spots, as they are called, from the shape which they generally take) along its sides, and sometimes it is not very easy for a beginner to tell whether a fish is a salmon or not. But the spots afford one a useful guide, and it is this: on the true salmon, and, of course, on the grilse, there are no spots below the medial line except two or three on the gill covers, and occasionally one or two close to the gill covers and just below the line.

Never gaff a kelt. Either tail or beach him. It is most important

that a kelt should be returned to the water unharmed to enable
him to return to the sea and the feeding grounds and return in due
course back to the river. . . . It is sometimes very difficult to tell
a well-mended kelt (that is to say one which has spawned some
time ago and has been feeding on his way down) from a salmon.
But the above notes may help you. One thing about a kelt is that
he will be forming teeth again

You will have gathered that only a very small proportion of
the little parr which went down to the sea ever survive to come
back as large salmon.

SEA LICE

A salmon with sea lice on it is fresh up from the sea—sea lice do
not live in fresh water for more than approximately 36 hours. The
sea louse has a waist and a sort of a tail and is shaped roughly like a
figure of eight with a tail. Thus:

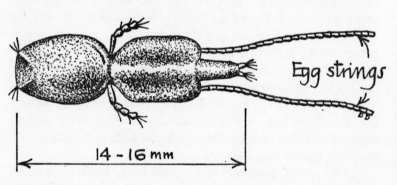

2. A female sea louse (*lepeophtheirus salmonis*). The male is 6–7mm long.

[2]

Fishing Tackle

Before we go on to the act of fishing, it is essential to know what we require to enable us to do so.

I would advise you to go to one of the shops where the man who serves you is himself a fisherman. I hope the following list will help you as to what to buy.

Quite a lot of gear can be made at home and it is great fun doing it—such things as priests, carriers, otters, gaffs etc., and you can learn to tie your own flies and lures—this is not nearly so difficult as some people think. Tying your own flies is well worth considering, if you are not very well off, because the price charged for made-up flies from shops is made prohibitive by the addition of tax. With a little application and a modicum of skill you can learn to tie your own flies quite adequately especially if you confine yourself to tying "hair" flies, as opposed to feathers. These hair flies work much better in the water and I am prepared to bet that in the next decade, most flies will be so tied. According to the original prescription there are fourteen different kinds of feathers in a Jock Scott. It is admittedly the most beautiful and quite one of the best killers of all salmon flies, but I doubt if the salmon would know or be any the less attracted if you left out 50 per cent of them. The flies tied with only hair (dyed of course) are not only very attractive and will catch fish but are much easier to tie. If you are going to tie your own flies, then you can do no better than get in touch with E. VENIARD, 138 NORTHWOOD ROAD, THORNTON HEATH, SURREY, from whom you can get all the necessary equipment. I would advise you to get the vice depicted in their catalogue. I would also suggest that you make

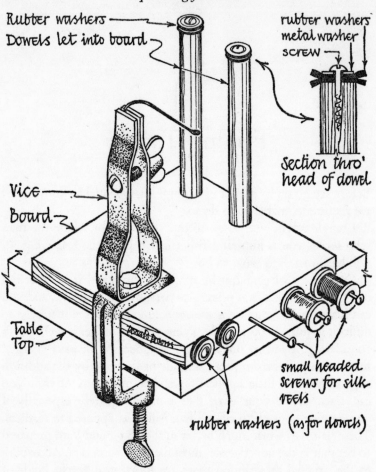

Rubber washers
Dowels let into board
Vice
Board
Table
Top

rubber washers
metal washer
screw

Section thro'
head of dowel

small headed
screws for silk
reels

rubber washers (as for dowels)

3. A fly-tying vice.

yourself a board ½in. thick and 12 × 6in. which can be secured to a table by the clamp of the vice, fig. 3. On this board you fit two or three wooden pillars, dowelled in firmly, about 3 to 4in. high. The top of these pillars must be filed in a smooth round and a small round circle of rubber (old motor inner tube) screwed on top. Several small buttons of rubber should also be screwed into the side of the board. You will find that when tying flies there are always several loose ends which if allowed to hang down, will get in the way. By means of these pillars and buttons you can use several silks and tinsels at a time and keep them out of the way. This is an idea of my own—at least I have never seen it used anywhere. Anyway it greatly helps and simplifies fly tying. You will of course require a pair of curved blade scissors. You can easily make your own bobbin-holders out of wire—a bottle stand is very useful for the varnishes and liquid waxes etc. (see Veniard's catalogue).

Excellent books on the subject that I know are: *Fly Tying— Principles and Practice* by Burrard, *Fly Dresser's Guide* by Veniard, and *Fly Tying Development and Progress* by Veniard and Downs. It is a fascinating hobby and will save you a lot of money. But do not be too ambitious.

NECESSITIES

Here I would add a word as to tackle. As the prize is large, powerful and greatly valued, so the tackle should be sound, strong and the best of its kind. Unfortunately, I am afraid, all these things will cost a good deal of money and it is well worth *insuring* them—which is a thing a great many people omit to do and when they have lost them or had them stolen, they find out to their regret, that they are not covered under their comprehensive policy. You can often pick up a good bargain at auction sales, but you *must* go with a friend who is an expert and who will advise you what to buy.

1. RODS

If you choose a rod, be sure that it is not a very whippy one. A rod that feels as if it had no backbone is a bad rod for salmon fishing.

And though a whippy rod undoubtedly has merits in the eyes of some anglers, there can be little doubt that it is the worst possible form of rod for the non-expert. He wants, not a heavy rod, not necessarily a stiff rod, but one with a quick, springy action, bending more at the top than in the butt. I have no hesitation in saying that if you can get hold of a good greenheart spliced vibration rod, you will never want to fish with anything else. The difficulty is this: no seasoned greenheart has come into this country since the war, so do not, whatever you do, buy a new one. Your only chance is to pick up an old one (provided the timber is still sound) or to pick up some pieces from broken rods and have them made up into a rod. There are still a number of firms able and willing to do this work reliably.

If you cannot get a greenheart vibration rod then I would recommend a spliced cane rod, as made by Sharpe's of Aberdeen —these are beautiful rods of a length from 12 to 13ft. As regards the length of a greenheart spliced vibration, I would recommend 15ft, but if you must have a smaller rod, say 13ft but not smaller— the smaller the rod the less benefit is derived from the vibration which is the secret of the rod. Some people will tell you that a 15ft vibration rod is too big and heavy—I have a 15ft, a 14ft and a 13ft rod and I am less tired after fishing all day with the 15ft for the reason that *the rod does all the work.* When you grow old and feeble, by all means take to a smaller rod, but I am imagining you to be young, big and strong. Also that you will hold the rod as instructed (see fig. 4) and not in the "backbreaking" style, which so many people do.*

These spliced rods do take a little longer to put up, but with a

* *Editorial note:* In recent years and after initial problems and much development, several rod makers have brought the fibreglass salmon rod up to a very high standard. One famous manufacturer has, indeed, now abandoned split cane and has produced a range of fibreglass rods which are, after you have mastered the timing, a pleasure to use. Fibreglass has the great advantage over cane and greenheart of being virtually indestructable and impervious to water. In the hands of an expert and with a line of the correct weight, these rods can not only cast a fly 40yds but have the right action for spey or switch casting. Like the author, I still, however, have a preference for spliced greenheart. The problem is to get hold of seasoned wood.

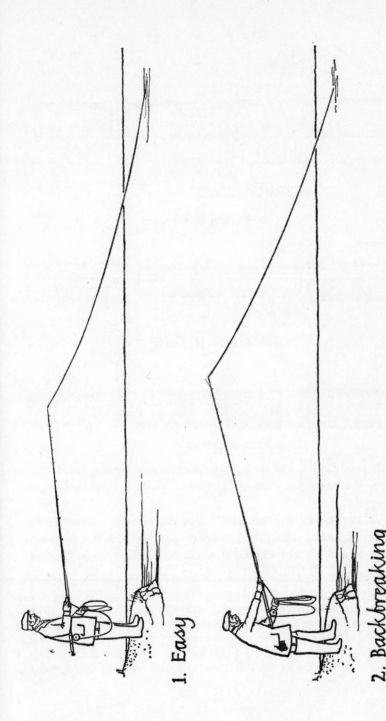

1. Easy

2. Backbreaking

4. Holding the rod.

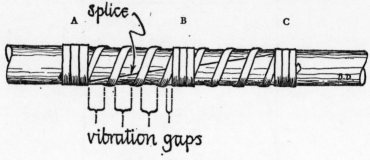

5a. Splice binding on vibration rod.

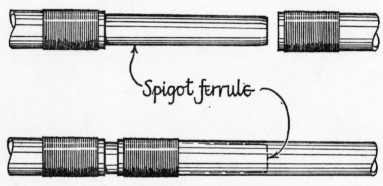

5b. Modern equivalent in fibreglass.

little practice you can do it very quickly. For binding use sticky tape—the best is ½in wide and brown in colour and can be bought in 25yd rolls.★

"GAPS" for vibration should be left. The best way to do this is to do the "GAPS" binding first, and then put three separate bindings at A B and C. Some people advocate binding with "leather

★ *Editorial note:* The author was evidently unfamiliar with spliced impregnated cane fly rods, now available in lengths of 12 to 15ft and deservedly popular. The impregnation bonds the bamboo sections into a solid structure which eliminates distortion and consequently separation of the sections. With these rods roll or spey casting is no more demanding than with spliced greenheart although the stiffer action requires different timing in casting and possibly a heavier line. Also greater care when playing a grilse with its relatively softer mouth.

thong", because they say that this is the only binding to give
VIBRATION to the rod. But I maintain that if bound properly with
tape (as per fig. 5) you will achieve this vibration, which admittedly
is all-important. Of course, if you cover the whole splice with
tape, as so many people do, there will be no vibration. By all
means use the leather-thong bound diagonally, if you find it best.
It is most important *not* to cover the whole splice with the binding. Bind diagonally leaving a *gap* between each bind; it is from
these gaps that you get the vibration which is all important.
Spliced rods are the only rods which will stand up to the Spey cast
for any length of time. When putting rods away in their canvas
covers, care should be taken never to do the tapes up tight. These
should be left quite loose or the fine tops of the rod may warp, if
put away for any length of time. At the end of the season rods
should be well cleaned and then given several coats of best varnish
and hung up in a cool dry place—always protect them well when
travelling—the tops and points are very vulnerable (see below).
Some of my friends have pointed out to me that a split cane rod is
stronger and tougher than a spliced vibration and is therefore more

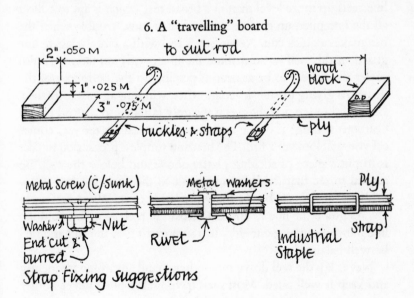

6. A "travelling" board

to suit rod

2" .050 M

wood block

1" .025 M

3" .075 M

buckles & straps

ply

Metal Screw (C/Sunk)

Metal Washers

Ply

Washer — Nut

End cut & burred

Rivet

Industrial Staple

strap

Strap Fixing suggestions

suitable for the beginner and also for taking abroad because the spliced vibration is more inclined to break and cannot be mended so easily. This I am prepared to admit but I will never agree that they are as nice to fish with. If you do use a split cane rod, always see that the ferrules are greased with mutton fat or tallow from an ironmonger—not oil, and never leave a rod up for any length of time and when putting it together see that the ferrules are clean, and also that the RINGS of any rod are clear of caked grease. This is often the case if the rod was used the season before for "greased line" fishing and had been put away without being properly cleaned.

2. REELS

Any reel of good make will do but it should be large enough to hold 30 to 40yds of No. 5 or 6 Kingfisher double tapered line and at least 100yds of backing. There are several very fine but very strong backings—I use terylene (25b/s), which is very fine but lasts for ever and is impervious to damp.

I prefer a narrow deep reel for "quick recovery" and also the line reels up more level than in a broad reel which is apt to collect all the line piled up on one side and may cause trouble when the fish makes a quick run. Never buy a reel with a circular agate line guard, as this will not distribute the line evenly on the reel. I also prefer the handle to be as near as possible to the periphery of the drum, so giving greater leverage when winding against resistance. Be careful to see that the reel is securely fastened to the rod before you start fishing; if in the excitement of the fight the reel comes off you will lose your fish. The best and simplest precaution to take is to put a piece of sticking plaster above and below the reel. Be careful to see that the line runs direct to the first ring and is not rubbing on the reel bar or the wrong side of it. When reeling in always guide the line to and fro across the reel, so as to avoid the line bunching up on one side. It is important that the rod and reel be well balanced.

Never lay the reel down on sandy ground: examine frequently and keep it well oiled. Most reels have brakes but I never bother about the brake but always use my thumb on the spool. When tending a reel, never stand over a hard surface (stone floor, road etc.), if the reel drops it will be damaged (see note on reels, page 67, suggesting a new kind of reel on the principle of the Silex spinning reel).*

3. FLIES

Many of the costly shop flies are so overloaded with feathers that when in the water they are only a sodden lump, and all life and movement is destroyed. These flies only begin to kill fish when they get old and are knocked to bits with use. Their proud owner, too, usually has a great tin box, or else a giant book, full of similar glories; and he spends a large part of his time, when he ought to be fishing, in inspecting these flies in order to decide which he shall use next, and then in tying it on in place of the one which he had last preferred.

Many fishers, after learning to make a cast, think that the flies are everything. There are some even who think that success is to be had only with double hooks, or with some fanciful short rising hook of monstrous shape. Still more salmon fishers, however, pin their faith to an endless variety of gorgeous flies with charming names—names that plainly speak their real use and object, that is, to catch the fisher, not the fish. These names are themselves a comedy.

Some are truculent, as Butcher, Bull-dog, Thunder and Lightning, Black Dose—carrying in their names the idea of triumphant compulsion brought to bear upon the unfortunate

* *Editorial note:* Some reels of contemporary design include sophisticated refinements such as slipping clutches and graded gears for speedy recovery of the line. I have several of them and have found them satisfactory for small summer fish on light tackle. But in big rivers and heavy water I prefer my old 4¼in. "Bernard" because of its robustness and simplicity of construction. This means that at times of stress or crisis there is no complicated mechanism to give you trouble. The late C. M. Wells who, fishing the same river in Norway from 1926–50 (with a break during the war years), used reels of the most simple design and with them killed his eightieth fish of over 40lbs on his eightieth birthday, all from the same river. This is a record which has never, to my knowledge, been equalled and which will certainly never be surpassed.

salmon. Others are romantic, as Fairy, Silver Grey, Green High-
lander, Golden Eagle, Snowfly, Kate. Others recall the deeds of
legendary heroes, such as Jock Scott, Popham, Wilkinson. Their
varieties, or supposed varieties, run into thousands, and the whole
lot show plainly that the fisher is even more gullible than the fish.

In truth, a good fisher with only half a dozen patterns of really
varied flies is, so far as catching salmon goes, not one whit behind
the man who arms himself with every fly and angling gadget that
the tackle shops will so cheerfully sell to him.

In my opinion, if a fly is neat and workmanlike, well-shaped,
and with wing and hackle dressed sufficiently lightly to play freely
in the water, it is of comparatively small importance of what
pattern or of what colours the various parts are composed. There
are, of course, points upon which some variety is obviously desirable. In big waters, or in waters stained with mud or with peat from
moorland streams, one instinctively feels that the fly should be
large and bright in order that it may be seen by as many fish as
possible. Salmon have wonderfully good sight at all times of the
day and night, and even in stained or muddy water (known as
"coloured") they can see the fly in an astonishing way. Still, if fish
are ever to be tempted to take the fly, the first essential is that they
should see it; and so one demands that flies shall be easy to see.

I should advise you not to pay overmuch attention to the
maxims current among salmon fishers as to what fly you should
use or what you should do in this event or in that. For instance,
you will be told, "always use big flies in spring, small flies in
summer and autumn"; "never cast again over a risen or pricked
fish until you have given him five minutes rest", or "have smoked
a pipe", or "have changed your fly for a smaller one", or "always
use bright flies on a bright day, dark flies on a dark day", and so on.
Now these maxims, and many more like them, are all very well.
They are well known and deeply revered amongst anglers, but I
often wonder whether the poor misguided salmon is always quite
sure of the path of duty thus laid down for him. As a general
maxim: when the water is very cold, it is desirable to use a large
fly so that it will sink low in the water—fish lie close to the bottom
in low temperature. In the summer, when the water is low, warm

and gin clear, it is obvious that a very small fly and light tackle should be used. A large fly dropped with a loud flop would obviously scare away rather than attract a fish. I think that if you provide yourself with different sizes of the following flies you will be adequately equipped for any river in the British Isles: Jock Scott, Thunder and Lightning, Logie, Blue Charm, Hairy Mary, Yellow Torrish, Silver Wilkinson, March Brown, Mar-lodge. Not too fully dressed. It is the size of the fly which matters most. As I said it is not easy to get flies properly dressed unless you make them yourself. This is not as difficult as you may think and it is very interesting and great fun and a great satisfaction to catch a salmon on your own make of fly. As I said before, many of the costly shop flies are much overloaded with feathers. I have recently gone in for hair dressed flies as opposed to feathers—they seem to work better in the water. Peter Deane of Eastbourne makes them professionally and does it very well.

HOOKS

As regards HOOKS I would strongly advise against DOUBLE hooks, except in the case of very small flies (size 3=1in. and smaller). The reason for this is that when a fish takes he invariably turns to go down and if he feels something awkward in his mouth, he will immediately try to get rid of it, whereas a single hook does not disturb him and he will *turn* with it still in his mouth. It is on this turn that you must drive the point of the hook into the scissors. (See HOOKING page 61).

As regards sizes of flies there is much confusion as there are several scales in use and one never knows, when someone talks of No.4 or No.4/0, which scale he is referring to—new numbers or old numbers or low water scale. Much the easiest and simplest way of describing the size is to do so in *inches*. The approximate size in inches of the scale most commonly used among fishermen is shown on the table overleaf. Therefore when asked what size of fly I am using I always say 1in. (No.3) or 2in. (No.5/0) etc. In this way there can be no misunderstanding. I would suggest having a card pasted in the lid of your fly case with scale marked in inches and numbers as shown on page 20.

ins.	nos.		ins.	nos.
3	9/0		$1\frac{3}{4}$	3/0
$2\frac{3}{4}$	8/0		$1\frac{1}{2}$	1/0
$2\frac{1}{2}$	7/0		$1\frac{1}{4}$	1
$2\frac{1}{4}$	6/0		$1\frac{1}{8}$	2
2	5/0		1	4
			$\frac{3}{4}$	6
			$\frac{5}{8}$	8

Note: When measuring the hook, only measure as far as the "EYE". Do not include it.

Note on LIGHTLY DRESSED FLIES. The late A. H. E. Wood (of Cairnton) even went so far as to fish with coloured hooks. No dressing!!

TUBE FLIES

While on the subject of flies, a mention should be made of TUBE flies, which are so much in use on some rivers. In fact if you attempt to fish on some rivers with anything else the ghillie may be contemptuous. The tube fly consists of a tube—the best are made of polythene and the hook is a triangle. The tube is dressed with hair, mostly stoat's tail and not feathers and in some cases is a very rough and ready job. There is no denying, they catch fish. My objection to them is the three hooks.

4. LURES

There are many lures and early on in the season when the water is high and liable to be coloured, they can be very deadly. The best lure I know is the "Yellow Peril" but there are many others—the Waddington, the General Practitioner etc. The Yellow Peril consists of two or three long yellow canary feathers on a 2 hook setting and the body covered with silver tinsel.

These are easily made and open to much experimentation.

7. Jock Scott. *Left*: fully dressed, *right*: lightly dressed.

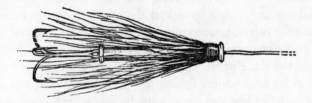

8. Stoat tail or other hairs.

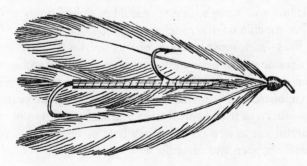

9. Yellow canary feathers and silver tinsel.

5. LINES

Although it will be rather costly, yet it is true economy to buy a really good line and then to keep it sound by seeing that it is invariably pulled out and dried after use, even though you intend to fish next day.

A double tapered Kingfisher No.5 or 6 is a good line for any normal salmon rod, except the very small rods which some people use, when a lighter double tapered line is necessary. There are many other kinds of fishing lines which I will not confuse you with at this stage, such as floating (bubble) lines etc. If you stick to the orthodox line, as suggested, you will be quite all right; but I must mention—an Air-Cel bubble line is very easy to fish with and eliminates all the bother of greasing your line—it "shoots" marvellously and is always ready for use—whereas so often the greased line may begin to sink at the precise moment when you feel sure the fish is about to take and you either have to reel in and regrease the line or risk fishing with a sinking line and a consequent drag on the fly. But we said we would not confuse the issue by going in for greased-line fishing just yet. But if you are going to use an Air-Cel line, which admittedly has so many advantages, non-drying, non-greasing and "putting away"—by all means do so. *But* remember when you are fishing in the early spring in ice-cold water and deep pools, where you want the fly to sink right down to the bottom, then it will be *no use at all*.

At the end of the season do not leave a line on the reel—the best way of keeping a line is to first of all clean it well. I usually rub the whole line with a rag with a very mild or light amount of "Cerelene" or mucilin or other such preparation that is sold for "greasing" lines—care must be taken not to overdo it. Then stretch it over a frame so that none of the strands touch one another and the air can get at them (see fig. 10, page 23). Hang the frame up in a cool cupboard and you will find the line will last for years in this way—otherwise it will get all tacky and sticky and be quite useless. Be careful not to step on a line in a boat or on a hard floor—this can easily happen and can ruin it.*

* *Editorial note:* For many years after the war it was not possible to buy in this

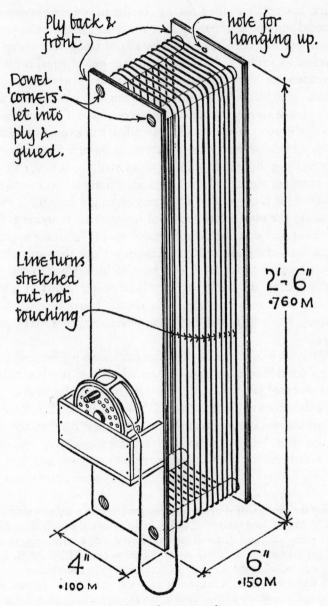

Ply back & front

hole for hanging up.

Dowel 'corners' let into ply & glued.

Line turns stretched but not touching

2'-6"
·760 M

4"
·100 M

6"
·150M

10. Frame for storing line.

6. NYLON

Nylon has revolutionised fishing. In the days before nylon was invented and one had to use gut, it was a very tricky business, but nylon, which besides having the benefit of being very cheap and therefore expendable, is far stronger than gut of equal thickness. It stretches and when you have a long line out and get caught in the bottom, as in bait fishing with an all nylon line, it sometimes takes quite a lot of energy to break it, that is of course if you are using a 15lb B/s or over, as one usually does when bait-fishing for salmon —it is seldom necessary to use anything lighter. The only snag with nylon is *knots*; no ordinary knot will do, it is apt to slip, you must use a double-blood knot for joining nylon to nylon, a ness knot for tying on flies and when making a loop tie it twice. These are the only knots you need know as far as nylon is concerned—I shall describe them on pages 39–44. Take care to get the best nylon—there are many makes—some not so good. One is always hearing about hard luck tales of broken nylon but it is usually because the knots have not been properly tied. It is quite amazing how many people, who should know better, still tie ordinary knots in nylon and these never do (see KNOTS pages 39–44).

Always retie or renew nylon after catching a big fish and never leave a wind knot in the cast—renew whole cast. It is best to have three spools of 50yds each of three different strengths (B/s) in your bag. I always carry (approx.) 20lb B/s, 15lb B/s, 10lb B/s. If fishing bait with nylon line, see that the cast is of a less B/s than the main line and then when you break either intentionally or otherwise you will break in the weakest part (cast) and not lose line. Of course if you are fishing in summer (bright) weather on rivers like

country the plastic-coated nylon-based fly lines now so readily available. My early "Ashaway" lines came from U.S.A. in the 1950s and are still in use. But in recent years U.K. manufacturers have developed such a wide range of these lines, graded for size according to the American code (HDH, HCH, GBG, GAG, etc), including the Wet Cel or Quick-sinking type, that you can fish the whole season with them in nearly all conditions. I say "nearly" because when casting against a strong wind nothing in my experience can penetrate it as well as a heavy silk line (e.g. No. 6 Kingfisher).

the Helmsdale or Oykel you will require much lighter B/s nylon
—say 7lb to 9lb B/s.

7. GAFFS

A most important and sadly neglected item in a fisherman's list of
necessities is the gaff. I have literally never seen the ideal gaff in any
of the many fishing tackle shops I have visited—they are either too
short and too narrow in the hook or too heavy and badly balanced
and therefore unwieldy and they nearly always have screwed on
hooks. If the hook is screwed on, sooner or later, and probably
just when you are actually into a fish, the screw will work loose
and the hook will turn and you will lose the fish and the hook.

The hook must be bound on firmly and the binding varnished.
If you are going to gaff your own fish and there is no question but
that this is far the best plan, for the very good reason that you are
the only person who can possibly know the exact and *precise
moment to act*; if you use the right sort of gaff, it is, with practice,
quite a simple job and you will hardly ever lose a fish at the gaff.
Whereas when you allow other people to gaff your fish I am
afraid you will have a number of disappointments; the ghillie or
the friend who attempts to gaff the fish for you *cannot possibly
know the precise moment that you wish him to stick the gaff in* and if you
try and tell him, you will only fluster and confuse him and he will
make a mess of it. I am not saying that there are not many ghillies
who are experts at this particular job but all I can say is that I have
seldom come across them and consequently I always prefer to gaff
my own fish, and I could count on the fingers of one hand the fish
I have lost at the gaff since I started gaffing them myself. As a
further argument in favour of this theory, I can say that I have
gaffed a good many fish for other people but never have the same
confidence in doing it as when I am gaffing my own and have
more than once missed the first time and had to have a second go.
So we will settle for gaffing your own fish. The best wood for the
gaff is well seasoned hazel—it is very light and very strong—the
right length is according to your height, 6ft or longer for a 6ft
man. I am 6ft 2in. and use a 7ft gaff. The pole should be as thin and
light as it can be, provided it is stiff and strong enough to act as a

wading stick, the bottom should be covered with lead which doesn't slip on rocks and which keeps the gaff right way up in the water when wading, and the hook should be of the best steel, not too thick and very sharp; the point will constantly have to be sharpened. The opening should be not too small, say 2½in. from A to B and 10in. from C to D. The shape also is important; the shape I like best is as per No. 1 (see fig. 11 page 29), some prefer as per No.2, but the fish is less likely to slip off No.1. At E there should be a metal or strong wire loop, firmly bound on.

You now have a gaff which you can use as a wading stick. You require a sling (cord or leather) which goes over one shoulder, attached to it is a short length of cord at the end of which is a "quick release" clip, as used on dog leads, which you clip on to the loop at E. The length of this cord is important; the correct length is so that when clipped on the gaff will hang comfortably at your side and when using it as a wading stick it is long enough to enable you to stretch out your arm. When you start casting you merely let it fall at your side. The hook should be protected by a rubber tube—those used on electric milking machines are the best—they are easy to remove and seldom fall off. It is just as well to unclip the gaff and remove the rubber tube a few minutes before you contemplate having to use the gaff (see page 80 "Catching a Fish"); by this time you will have made up your mind, or at any rate you should have done, where on the river bank you intend to bring the fish in to the gaff. Incidentally, while on this point, if you are fishing alone and going to gaff your own fish, before starting to fish a pool you should examine the bank for possible gaffing places, that is to say, see that there is some place (or places) clear of branches and roots in the water. Never try to gaff him when you are yourself still in the water. He may get tangled up with your legs. You will usually find a soft place in the bank where you can implant the gaff, hook upwards, leaving both hands free to work the rod. When fishing with a long rod there is a terrific bend on it when bringing a fish close in to the gaff and this means a great strain on the top joint. A good tip at this point is to take off 2 or 3ft of slack line (not on the reel) and hold this slack in the usual manner, with the fingers of the left hand, against the rod in a loop. This slack should be gently released immediately the fish is on the gaff. Of course if you release this slack too quickly the point will "spring" back and may break. The rod point will then at once resume the straight and the strain is released. Always try bringing the fish in from right to left, no matter which way the river runs. In this way, with the rod held in the left hand and the gaff in the right, your gaff will not run over the line—a most risky performance and one which has lost many a fish. Never bring the fish into shallow water if this can be avoided. The reason is obvious. As long as the whole fish is underwater, it is not disposed to be restless, but when brought into shallow water where it becomes partially uncovered by its natural element, it is apt to be restless, for the very reason that the oxygen obtainable in the air, when the head is out of the water, will REVIVE him. Never raise the fish's head out of the water. Never gaff a fish when he is "END ON" to you. Now PLACE the gaff over his back, as near the middle as you can, never JERK it in but IMPLANT it firmly, at the same time raising the gaff towards you and upwards and releasing the 2 or 3 ft of slack. It is wise to retreat a yard or two from the river bank before killing the fish, so that if anything untoward happens and he comes off the gaff before you have killed him, he will not fall back into the river. You now place the rod gently on the bank, taking care never to put the reel down on a sandy place. Care should be taken when putting the rod down on the bank to see that the reel is uppermost, so that if anything happens and the fish gets off the gaff before you have killed him, the line will run free. If you have released the 2 or 3 ft of slack, there will be no tension between the rod top and the fish. Never release the fish off the gaff before you have administered the *coup de grâce* with a priest (see fig. 12, page 31) which you should have in your right hand pocket —there may not be a suitable stone or stick to hand.

It may seem to you rather unnecessary to make all this fuss about gaffing a fish, but it is by no means the least important part of catching a fish, and as I said before, it is a part which is sadly neglected. It is not too easy to hook a salmon and so if you are lucky enough to do so, why not make sure of landing him safely. It is therefore well worth while taking all this trouble to do so, but very few people do and consequently many a good fish is lost at the gaff. One often hears hard luck stories about big fish (they are always big ones!) being lost at the gaff, but if you only knew the truth you can be quite certain that there was something wrong somewhere; either failure to observe these rules or the use of a faulty weapon. I will guarantee that if you will take the trouble to follow the above instructions and use the right sort of gaff, you will lose very few fish at the gaff. I would once again strongly recommend you always to GAFF your own fish.*

There are several other methods of landing a fish: (a) by landing net, (b) by tailer, (c) by beaching, but none of them are nearly as good or as safe as gaffing. The trouble is, fishmongers object to gaffed fish and that is the main reason why people use other means—a purely monetary reason, and not worthy of a fisherman's consideration.

(a) LANDING NET

This is all very well if you have a ghillie to carry it for you or if you are fishing from a boat. It is quite impossible to wield the thing yourself because it has to be large and therefore heavy in order to be able to get the big fish into it. But if you do use a net see that it is sound. The netting perishes and if this occurs you will lose the fish. Here I would advise you never to try and net a fish over 20lb.

(b) TAILER

This is a good weapon and with practice can be used quite successfully on many occasions, but *not all*. There are circum-

---

* *Editorial note:* I do not share the author's enthusiasm for the gaff which I never use except for large spring fish in heavy water, e.g. on the Wye in March and April. I carry a net for small summer fish and for grilse but always beach them when they can be brought to a shelving beach. Admittedly you must play the fish longer and never attempt to walk it into the bank until it has turned on to its side. Once the head and shoulders are out of the water the fish will not stir until you touch it. So you have ample time in which to lay your rod down, then, getting into the river beyond the fish, either heave it ashore up the bank or grasp the root of the tail with one hand and insert a couple of fingers into the gills and carry it ashore. I have lost fish from the gaff and at the point of netting, but never by beaching.

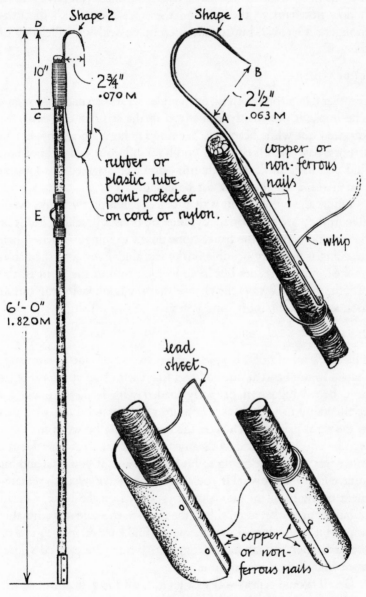

Shape 2

Shape 1

D

10"

C

2¾"
.070 M

2½"
.063 M

A

B

rubber or
plastic tube
point protecter
on cord or nylon.

copper or
non-ferrous
nails

whip

E

6'-0"
1.820M

lead
sheet

copper
or non-
ferrous nails

II. Gaffs.

stances where a tailer is of no use at all and, if on these occasions, it is the only weapon you have with you, then you have had it. It does not damage the fish and therefore meets with the fish-monger's approval, but it cannot compare with the efficiency of the gaff.

(c) BEACHING

A rather dangerous method, even under ideal beaching conditions. The hook, if not firmly embedded in the scissors, can easily be knocked out while beaching. See notes *re* hooking a fish—not in scissors, page 62. Of course if you have left your gaff behind and find you have to beach your fish—don't be alarmed—as long as you are on a suitable bank for beaching.

I think the whole point is that it all depends on the banks available. If they are steep or rocky, then obviously beaching is out of the question. But if the banks slope down to shingle beaches then beaching is not only possible but practicable. Even so if the fish is hooked, not in scissors but in top or bottom of the front of the mouth, there is always the chance that the hook will drop out as soon as the "strain is off" and you may lose your fish.

8. PRIEST

The best kind of priest is a piece of hardwood about 6 to 8in. long, shaped to the hand at one end and filled with lead at the other. It need be no bigger, if properly loaded with lead, than will go comfortably in your pocket (see fig. 12). One good tap with this in the right place, which is on the head exactly between the eyes, will be enough to deal with any fish—but take care he doesn't move just as you are going to hit him because, if you miss and hit yourself, you'll know it! If you are like me, you may, in the excitement of the moment put your priest down on the bank, instead of into your pocket after killing the fish—in this case it is advisable to paint it white, it is so much easier to find later on in the grass or bracken where it may have dropped. All mine are painted white, since when I have not lost one.

Here I would repeat—NEVER let him off the gaff or out of the net before administering the *coup de grâce*.

12. A priest.

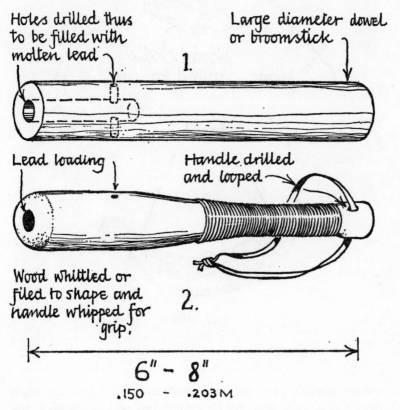

Holes drilled thus to be filled with molten lead

Large diameter dowel or broomstick

1.

Lead loading

Handle drilled and looped

Wood whittled or filed to shape and handle whipped for grip.

2.

6" – 8"
.150 – .203 M

9. CARRIERS

A thick piece of cord (or leather) with a bent meat hook at one end and a long loop at the other makes a good carrier; better still if the cord is threaded through a cylindrical block of wood (fig. 13). Without a carrier a salmon can be an awkward thing to carry and two salmon more so.

The hook goes into the scissors and the loop over the tail. If you have no carrier one can easily be extemporized with some thick cord. Pass cord through mouth and out at the gills and tie knot. With other end tie slip knot round tail. Adjust this to be as short as possible to avoid fish dragging on ground.

If ever you are lucky enough to catch so many salmon that you

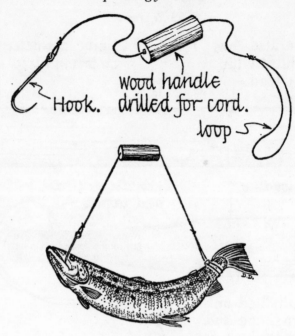

13. A carrier.

cannot possibly carry them all, remember that fish in the water weigh practically nothing. Of course this will not help if you have to carry the fish across country, but if the problem is to get the fish back to the fishing hut which is presumably on the river bank, then a good plan is to thread a stout line (see "Musts" page 38) through their gills and float them down or even up the river. This is not nearly as mad as it sounds and has often been done. The fish (several of them) will float downstream easily and can even be pulled upstream—if the current is not too strong—anyway it is a lot easier than carrying them.

10. SCALES

You want some good spring scales, capable of weighing up to 50lb—get the best.

II. OTTERS

An otter is a device to free the tackle when it becomes caught up in the bottom. Otters are used more in spinning, where if you are fishing properly (in certain conditions), you should be fishing deep or with the bait very near the bottom. You will, in certain rivers, constantly be hung up on the bottom, and even when fishing deep with fly one is sometimes caught up.

All you need are some split key rings and some string, any bit of old dry driftwood on the bank will do. You want a stick about 15in. long—attach the key ring to the middle of a piece of string about 2ft 6in. long and then tie each end firmly to the ends of the stick, thus forming a triangle—slip the line through the split ring and chuck it in and let it float down below where the snag is and then pull up. With practice (and it is quite fun doing this), you will be able to extract the hooks from most snags. The size of the key ring is important; if you have a key ring large enough to go right over the wings of the bait, then it will go right down to the triangle hooks and this is the secret, because then you get a really good pull on the very place you require it, namely, exactly where you are

14. An otter.

stuck. Whereas if the ring does not go over the wings of the bait, the pull will not be in the right place and may even embed the hooks deeper in the snag. You may think that you will lose the otter if the ring is large enough to go over the bait wings, but in fact you don't often do so and even if you do it is an expendable item, the only cost being the ring, and you still save the fly or bait.

12. WADERS

In cold weather an extra pair of socks pulled over the feet of your stockings is a good thing to keep you warm, and so is pulling the stocking tops over one's knees instead of turning them down, as is commonly done. Personally in very cold weather in early spring, when ice is about, I always wear a pair of long thick fisherman's stockings which I put on over my own stockings and pull them right up over the knees, over my plus fours up to my thighs. They can be got in almost any fishing town on the EAST coast of Scotland, Aberdeen, Montrose, etc. Quite apart from fear of cramp to come, it is worth while to keep warm because it makes fishing so much more pleasant, and because, if you keep your legs warm, your hands will not so easily get to that pitch of numbed stiffness familiar to every salmon fisher when no knot can be tied, and when, at the end of the day, the return of warmth to fingers can almost make you dance with pain.

Great controversy rages as to whether you should or should not wear a strap round your waist when wading in dangerous waters. Many anglers assert that if you do use a belt and do not allow the water free entry into your waders and have to swim for your life, the buoyancy of your legs will drown you by causing your head to go under water and your feet to bob about on the surface like corks. I have even met men who claim to have seen this happen. Well, that is all utter nonsense. A salmon fisher who has been swept away by the stream may be stunned or numbed by having his head or his limbs struck hard against a boulder, or he may be dazed by the sudden cold and by the knocking about he gets when he is trying to struggle to his feet in a swift current that is tumbling him along down the stream, but he has no need to fear the result of having air in his waders. His feet will not bob about on the surface or sink his head. It has been tried more than once by deliberately falling out of a boat when crossing the river in waders, and the result is nothing of the sort. The buoyancy is enough to keep your legs well up, but it does not bother you at all, and you swim quite easily, although the clumsiness of the waders makes you very slow. But if the waders do fill with water it makes it difficult to get out if the bank is high. Indeed, when the legs of the waders do fill with water it becomes much harder to swim, although you can do it well enough if you swim carefully and keep calm and go with the stream. The real danger is that when you slip in heavy water you struggle to recover yourself and get greatly knocked about and flustered in the attempt to regain your footing or to reach the bank at the point where you fell in. If you have to wade back to a point upstream in a strong current, DO NOT ATTEMPT TO TURN ROUND; it is far easier to keep one's footing with the rush of water coming from behind. Similarly if one has to cross a stream ALONE it is better to side-step with one's back to it.

You cannot be too careful when you have to cross swift, glassy currents. They are generally much stronger than they look, and when the river is rising you must be specially careful in such places—one inch more water may make them ten times more dangerous. Always use a stout staff or gaff with which to steady yourself and to feel your way in heavy water, but if two of you have to cross dangerous water or a rising river, go in together walking abreast (facing *across* the stream), and let each with one hand grip fast the shoulder of the other at arm's length. Wading so, you support each other, and you can cross water where one man alone would be swept away; the upper wader breaks the force of the current and is himself supported by the lower one.

Not only when you have to cross the stream, but always when you are wading in big waters, unless the weather has been absolutely settled, you should be on the look-out for any rising of the river. In most rivers that have their source amongst the mountains a sudden rise of the water may occur at the most unexpected time. Heavy rain overnight and many miles away from you, or a thunderstorm amongst the hills, may fill the mountain streams, and many hours later when you are fishing, with no idea of what is coming, the river will suddenly rise and give you precious little time to make yourself safe. The first signs that you will see are little straws, chips and dry leaves floating by, and if you look at the edges of the gravel bed the water begins to swell up round the dry stones, as in a cup that is brimming over, in a way that is unmistakable. But when you see those straws and bits of grass floating by, look about you, and make sure that your retreat is safe; a rising salmon river may be a very dangerous thing, and many of them rise very fast. I always put a stick at water level on the bank when I start fishing a pool—this will tell you if the river is rising or falling.

Nothing destroys waders more than carelessly tugging and tearing at them to get them inside out, and you should be very sure of the people who may have to do this for you. It is an owner's job.

There is often some difficulty in getting the foot of each wader turned inside out without forcing it, but this can be done by the *air-pressure* alone if the waders, when turned inside out as far as the ankles, are rolled down from the upper end in a tight roll. This forces the compressed air into the feet, which will then turn inside out of their own accord. Too easy.

As laces for your brogues you will find nothing better than a bit of common plaited blind cord.

The socks that are worn over the waders, to protect them from being cut or rubbed through by the sand and small stones that get into your brogues, should be good thick ones. It is a good plan to have the soles of these socks double knitted, or else roughly darned with coarse wool to about twice the ordinary thickness, and they will then last very much longer, and your waders will do the same. These socks should not be so long that they hang down over the boots. A pocket in the top of the waders is a MUST.

The best waders I know are called "Blackface". They are not heavy, they have a shiny surface and consequently are immediately dry on getting out of the water—a great boon. I recommend felt (double) soles and well nailed heels for the brogues, which should be *boots* not shoes. These are not by any means the only good waders—some of the latest are made with the boots attached which saves brogues and outside socks—these I believe are very good but I have never tried them.

Thigh waders—the best I know are "ALTONA". But some people prefer light waders (thigh high) in brogues. For women, Canadian thigh waders are recommended.

13. MACKS

Nearly everyone hates fishing in a mack and I am sure it is because of condensation caused by lack of ventilation. A fishing mack should have a slit (vent) at the back, running from shoulder blade to shoulder blade. This will do away with condensation. If you are wading deep you will want a short mack which will button up by means of press buttons into a yet shorter mack, so as to avoid trailing in the water when wading deep. A mackintosh hat is very useful, especially if it keeps the water from running down your neck. Mackintosh trousers in a boat are essential. It is no good keeping the legs dry if your seat is wet.

As regards clothes—never go out fishing in thin flannels. Thick rough tweed is best. Plus fours and a loose coat and good pull-overs, long flannel pants and string vests. A leather (sleeveless) waistcoat or Husky. A pair of leather backed (shooting) mittens and thin rubber surgical gloves are recommended. It is the wet that makes your hands cold and you cannot fish in woollen gloves. A good muffler is a MUST. These remarks, of course, refer to fishing in early spring when the water is ice-cold.

14. FLY BOXES

There is no need to buy expensive fly boxes. They nearly all have metal clips which you are supposed to clip the hooks under— these often knock the fine points of the barb off and if any damp gets in (and how can you avoid this when fishing?) then the hooks get rusty and break. The best kind of fly box is any old tin of required size, with felt or thick flannel, or better still, thin foam rubber glued in. You can then stick the hooks in and tear them out —no harm done to the points—no rust—no expense (see page 20 *re* card with scale of fly sizes glued inside box). Always take a small fly box or several suitable flies in your hat when wading, so as to avoid coming out when you have flicked the fly off or wish to

change it. If you are wading deep it is a bore to have to come out—
but great care should be taken, if you do this, not to drop anything
in the water!

Always leave the box open after fishing to air and dry any of the
damp flies. Hair flies dry much quicker than feathers.

15. ET CETERA

Scissors. You will require a good pair of scissors which should have
blunt tips in the form of pliers. These should be attached by a cord
or leather strap to your person.

Bag. A good waterproof fishing bag to contain everything you
require out fishing. The great mistake here is to have too small a
bag. By advising a big bag, I do not mean that you should take a
lot of unnecessary junk down to the river. You will learn in time
what is needed for a day's fishing. But by having a large enough
bag you can get the extra light mac or pullover in. At the foot of
this page I have appended a list of MUSTS.

Anti-Midge. A bottle of anti-midge stuff is essential on some rivers.

Thermometer. An anglers pocket thermometer is also essential. It is
important to know the temperature of the water and the air (see
notes on TEMPERATURE on page 71).

Disgorger. A disgorger is very useful—sometimes it is almost impossible to get the fly (and more so the bait) out, if the fish has
swallowed it. Kelts often swallow the fly or bait.

File. A small file for sharpening hooks and barbs. A small Carborundum stone is best.

String. A ball of string or fine cord is useful for many things, e.g.
floating fish, making otters etc.

Bag. The following is a list of "Musts" for your bag:

(1) Small fly box, with selec-
tions "for the day" from your
other fly boxes.

(2) Spools (50yds) Nylon 10lb,
15lb and 20lb B/s.

(3) Scales

(4) Disgorger

(5) Carrier (better take two)

(6) Anti-midge

(7) Thermometer

(8) Ball of string

(9) Three or four split key rings

(10) Two spare rubber tubes for
gaff

(11) File

(12) Small flask of whisky

16. KNOTS

Do not be confused by trying to learn a lot of complicated knots. Nylon needs special knots, none of the ordinary knots will do— they are apt to slip. But you need only learn a few knots.

(1) The Double Blood knot—Nylon to nylon—this is the best and tidiest knot in the world. It is essential to learn this knot (see fig. 15).

(2) The "Riddle" knot—for tying on flies. This knot is probably known by other names, but I never saw it until taught it by my ghillie on the river Ness (D. R. Riddle). It is the simplest and the best knot for tying on flies and can easily be tied in the dark or in a gale—(see fig. 16 (1) (2) (3)).

(3) The Loop—A simple loop but in nylon this *must* be tied *twice*.

(4) Loop to Line (or Cast to Line). A figure of 8 (see fig. 17, page 43).

(5) Joining Line to Backing—Whipped on (see fig. 18, page 43).

(1) *Double Blood Knot*

The knot is tied thus:

(1) Lay the two ends side by side and about ⅛in. apart, holding them in your left hand at C by the first finger and thumb, the end of the left hand strand being nearer to your body.

(2) With your right hand take the nearer end and wind it three times round the other strand—winding over and away from you.

(3) Then bend it back and poke it up between the two strands where your left thumb is at C. Do NOT tighten yet—this is half the knot done—the other half consists in doing exactly the same

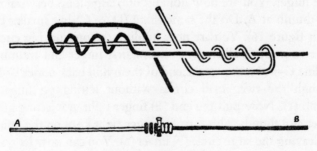

15. A Double Blood Knot.

thing with the opposite half of the knot.

(4) Shift the half knot, as it stands, from your left hand into finger and thumb of right hand at C.

(5) Take the loose end and bring it over the long strand towards you and so wind three times round the long strand, winding under and away from you.

(6) Then bend it back and poke it down between the two strands at C, so as to lie beside the other loose end, but pointing in the opposite way.

The knot is now ready to tie. Moisten left finger and thumb and with them hold the knot lightly at C, while you pull the two ends A & B firmly—the knot will now turn up into a compact and complete roll, with the two ends sticking out at right angles (see D).

In tying the blood knot, it must be remembered that the two ends must be twisted in opposite directions in order to get the twist continuous or the knot will be spoilt; for the knot is nothing more than two strands twisted together for six complete turns and then having the loose ends brought back to the centre and stuck through this twist in opposite directions.

(2) " Riddle" Knot

Thread cast through eye of fly and then fling it up the cast and forget about it altogether until you have tied the knot. Now hold the nylon at A between first finger and thumb of left hand. Make a large loop F bringing loop back between finger and thumb over line at A. You should grip this large loop in your palm with little finger. You are now holding one large loop between finger and thumb at A. Do the same thing (D & C) but smaller circles (as in figure 16). You are now holding the original big circle (F) and two more small circles between first finger and thumb over the line G–B. Now pass the end of the nylon back under G–B but through the two small circles without letting go finger and thumb (1). Now pull the end (E) finger tight, not letting go with finger and thumb. This forms a finger tight knot on the line G–B but leaving the large circle (F) intact (2). You can now let go with finger and thumb of left hand—now put first finger and thumb

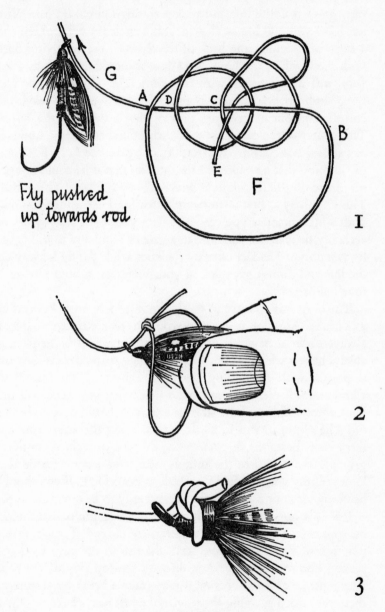

Fly pushed
up towards rod

16. A "Riddle" Knot.

of right hand through the large loop and sliding fly down the cast, grasp it amidships and pull it through circle (F) (2). With left hand you pull line at G slowly, the circle (F) will tighten and a knot will form at the back of the fly with the end lying flush with the shank of the hook, see (3), as it should do. The fly rides very well in the water with this knot. This matter of the end lying flush with the shank is important—some knots leave the end sticking out or even up, thus causing a ripple in the water. This matter of the cast *lying in line* with the shank of the hook (as in 3 above) was considered so important by the late A. H. E. Wood of Cairnton that he expressed the opinion that if he could not get his cast to do this he might as well "give up fishing"! This is bad. This knot may at first seem complicated but I can assure you that with a little practice you can tie it with your eyes shut—you can certainly tie it in the dark and in a gale of wind and it will never let you down. The fact of tying the knot while the fly is away up the line and cannot get stuck in your finger or in your clothes is much in its favour.

The only way to learn to tie this knot (or any other knot) is to PRACTISE. As nylon is so cheap, you can treat it as expendable. I always order a new lot of nylon each year and consequently always have a whole lot of old nylon going spare. This is the stuff to practise with. A good tip when practising to tie this knot is to allow yourself plenty of nylon, so that when you have tied the knot, there will be at least 1ft over at E, which will have to be cut off. The object of this is, so that when tying the knot, you can more easily bring the three circles A, B and C over the first finger, gripping them against the thumb. When you come to tie this knot skilfully you will find very little to cut off at E. If you should be changing your fly often, this is obviously to be recommended.

It is now important to point out what the length of cast should be. This must be regulated by the length of the rod; if you have too long a cast, then, when you bring the fish to the gaff, the knot joining line to cast may come through the top ring of the rod. This must be avoided because it may cause a break by jamming, therefore, when assessing the length of a cast never have it longer than two joints of your rod.

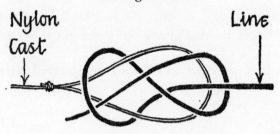

17. Line to cast.

A double loop on nylon cast—a simple figure of 8 with line, as in figure.

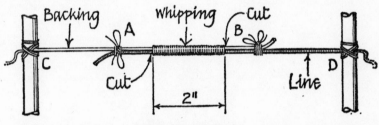

18. Line to backing.

This must not be done by means of any knot, because a knot will not travel smoothly through the rings, when playing a fish. The line must be WHIPPED (or spliced) on to the backing in such a way as to look and feel like a continuous line. The best method is to lay about 6in. of line against a similar length of backing and then tie a firm knot at A and B, 6in. apart, with a strong piece of twine, then attach the backing firmly to some immoveable object at C, and the line to some immoveable object at D, pulling A–B as tight as possible. You now have both hands free for the WHIP-PING. First apply some cobblers wax or liquid wax to the line and backing between A and B—now take some strong silk and, after waxing it well, commence to bind the two together for about 2in. between A and B—you must go up and down the line several times, applying the liquid wax to the whipping each time. Finish off in the usual way of binding and cut off the two loose ends and the two bits of twine at A and B. Later apply two coats of varnish.

Another method is to wind the two lines round each other between A and B—thus giving more strength to the join after waxing well.

The time has now arrived when we must proceed to learn how to fish.

[3]

Casting

The normal fault with some beginners is that they fail to *bend* the rod; they use it not as a whip but as if it were a stiff pole. In their effort to send the line back behind them they throw the point of the rod too far back. They wave the rod back, instead of first raising the line to the surface of the water, by lifting the rod top gently, and then sharply throwing the line back and up into the air behind them, with a flip of the top of the rod. You should always start your learner in a swift, even-running stream, where his line will be *pulled out* taut for him by the current before each new cast is made. The act of casting with a salmon rod is a straight overhead flip-flip, that is, a strong flip back and upwards; then a sharp and firm stopping of the rod whilst you may count steadily one, two; then a much easier flip forward and upward. The tempo of the count has to be assessed by the length of line in the air.

The Detail of Overhead Casting (see fig. 19 pages, 48–49).
Before the cast begins the rod must be raised, usually to an angle of about 45° from the water, in order to bring the line to the surface before you try to throw it back behind you. No rod can throw back a line which is still left *sunk deeply* in the water, except as a very occasional effort and in the hands of a skilled fisher.

For ordinary fishing the line must be brought as near the surface as possible before each cast.

Again, when the flip-flip has been given, the rod point is still high in the air and is allowed to sink almost in one movement to an easy position in which it may be held whilst the fly swings round behind. The novice often fails to see that the *force* is all put into the *very beginning* of the forward flip. If he merely waves the rod forward, his line follows the downward direction and falls in a heap.

Consider by itself the act of throwing the line forward. As you want a line, at that moment stretching back from the rod top, to be thrown straight forward over the water, it is easy to see that the impetus must be given at the highest part of the curve made by the rod, for that alone can give the line a forward pull parallel to the water level. Similarly, after making the backward flip, which is to lift the line, the rod should instantly be stopped firmly with the butt piece very little past the perpendicular—of course the top will bend back rather more. Even so, the line is falling as it runs out behind you, but if the rod is waved far back, as novices almost always do, the line is dragged downwards and cannot extend behind you. It is essential that it should extend behind as far as possible in order to prepare for a clean and easy cast forward.

In describing the cast both back and forward again you notice that I say that it should be a flip backwards and upwards, and forwards and slightly upwards. This is the key to good casting. As the backward flip is made, the wrists and elbows are raised so that the lower of your two wrists is almost shoulder high. Then as the line runs back, the rod, almost unconsciously, is allowed to sink 6 or 8in. perpendicularly and as the forward flip is given the elbows are again raised, and the point of the rod, as it were, pushed out forward and upward moving the whole body with a much slower and slighter flip than the backward one.

Even when you have learned to cast well you will often, at the beginning of the season, or when getting tired, find that your casting is not pleasing you, is not so straight and easy as it should be and that the fly is not falling at the full stretch of the cast. Then is the time to remember to use your wrists and raise them high, and as it were to lift the flip back and aim the forward cast higher. You will find that all your old skill and lightness have returned.

An overcast cast, then, is made thus (beginning from the fishing position at the end of the former cast, see fig. 19):

(1) Take in some slack and raise the rod slowly to bring the line to the surface, then (without any pause)

(2) A sharp flip back and up, raising the arms and stopping the rod

sharply when the butt is just beyond the upright. This must be done over the right or left shoulder, not straight up. If you bring the rod back "straight up" the fly will most likely hit the rod and break the point.

(3) A pause of about a second to allow the line to extend to the rear, then an easy flip forward and upward. (During the pause the rod sinks perpendicularly a few inches, and in the forward cast the arms are fully outstretched and level with the shoulders.)

(4) Then the rod, without a pause, gently sinks to the fishing position, and the arms are drawn in to the sides.

The chief difficulty with a novice is to master the timing of the cast. He will hardly ever give the line time to run out behind him before making the cast forward. With an average length of line, say about three or four rod lengths out from the reel to the fly, the time is this (spoken slowly)—lift, then FLIP—one—two—flip—and lower.

I need hardly say that when you become skilful you can choose amongst many styles of casting, and in each style can fish with much variation; but when once you have mastered the *simple overhead cast*, as it is called, you can fish almost any pool perfectly well, and soon other ways of casting will come to you naturally and easily. But you must first learn to do the simple cast over *both* shoulders—and not straight up.

Casting against a high wind blowing almost straight in his face is a severe trial to a beginner. His fly will persist in falling back in a muddle just when the cast seemed about to uncurl and fall at its full stretch. He puts more and more force into the cast and quickly gets tired and disheartened. He should go at it *not violently* but more quietly, should throw the line rather on to the surface of the water than over it as usual, and should finish his cast with the rod top actually touching the water. He should cast quietly but cast, as it were, at the water, and he will soon find that he can cast even against such a wind quite comfortably and quite well. But a good rod is a great help to him. Finally to sum up in short—pull in some line before picking the line off the water, then raise the point of the rod until there is a quantity of line off the water (see 1). Then bring the rod back fast (vigorously) and high but not

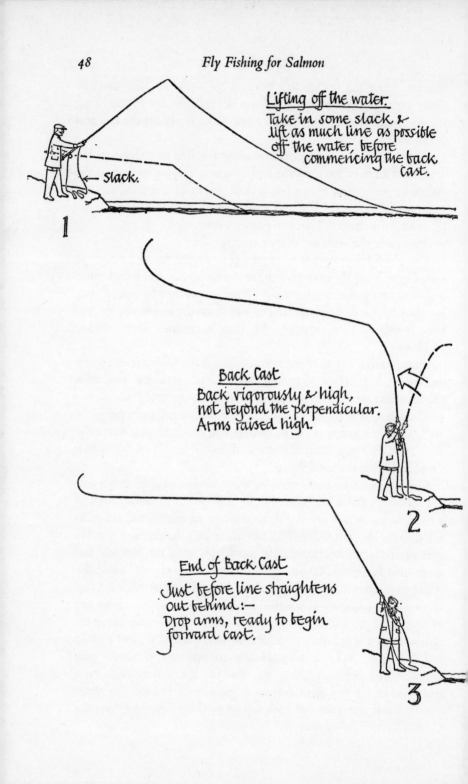

Lifting off the water.
Take in some slack &
lift as much line as possible
off the water, before
commencing the back
cast.

← slack.

1

Back Cast
Back vigorously & high,
not beyond the perpendicular.
Arms raised high.

2

End of Back Cast
Just before line straightens
out behind :—
Drop arms, ready to begin
forward cast.

3

Forward Cast

"Push" rod vigorously forward and upwards, moving whole body forward; arms raised again – aiming at a point well above water – and shooting slack.

Slack

4

End of Cast

Arms dropping – let fly 'unfold' gently on the water. Slack all shot.

5

19. Overhead casting.

beyond the perpendicular (see 2), raising both arms in doing this. If the fly leaves the water with a distinct PHUT noise you can then usually rely on making a good forward cast, provided that you time the forward cast properly. If you find it necessary to drop the rod beyond the perpendicular in order to get the line off the water, then do not attempt a forward cast, but make a false cast on to the water, away from the fishing area. Immediately the line touches the water—before it has a chance to sink and drown—pick it up, it will come up easily if it is still on top of the water. Then cast again according to above instructions. Many people make a false cast on nearly every occasion and you will find it most necessary if the water on your side of the river is slack or, as is so often the case, a backwater.

Timing is the great thing—begin the forward cast precisely just

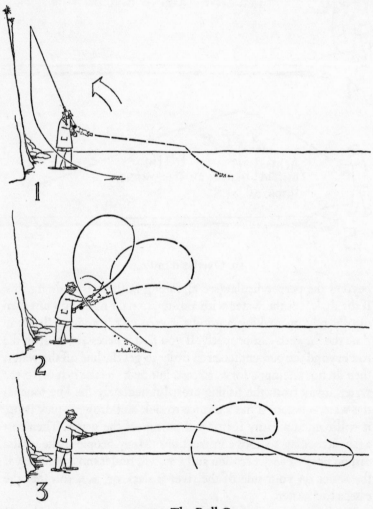

20. The Roll Cast.

as the line straightens out behind you and not before it does—see (3). At this point your arms should have dropped a few inches.

Now PUSH the rod vehemently forward and upwards (4), moving your whole body forward and aiming at a point some way above the point in the water where you wish to drop the fly. It will then billow out the line and the fly will fall beautifully on the water (5), your arms returning to the fishing position. When you have learnt to do this then you can start to SHOOT line—this means that at a given point you release the line held in a loop in the left hand, which you gathered up at the beginning of the lift off the water, thus greatly extending the length.

It is most important to examine the hook and the barb from time to time, if you are fishing with rocks behind you. Don't forget the file for sharpening hooks—and finally, never try to cast a longer line than you can control. It is only *showing off* and seldom pays. Remember—by fishing a short line you can have much more control and can "hang" your fly in the stream.*

* *Editorial note:* THE ROLL CAST. (see Fig 20) As the author has omitted this fairly simple but indispensable method, the artist Donald Downs offered to illustrate the basic technique. The overhead cast cannot be used when the fisherman finds himself with a high obstacle behind him, e.g. a tree, a high bank or a rock face. He must therefore employ a method which does not bring the fly behind him. Hence the need for the Roll or Switch Cast.

To make it effectively in a strong current the line must be brought by a false Roll Cast into a position opposite the fisherman. The drawings show the essential movements and I merely add that the Roll Cast can be made successfully with a cane, greenheart or fibreglass rod, providing that whichever is used is reasonably flexible and not too stiff. Once the timing is mastered it is possible to shoot line just as far as with the overhead cast. But, as in all forms of fly-casting, the line must first be brought to the surface. You cannot roll-cast a sunk line.

WHERE TO CAST

Now as to the direction of your cast. Your books will tell you to cast down and across the stream and at an angle of about 45°; and so you should do in straightforward, simple streams, where such a cast will enable you to put your fly well beyond the lie of the fish. But never hesitate to vary the angle to suit any pool. Especially in swirling pot holes or in any pool where there is a strong eddy on one or both sides, a cast made straight across or even slightly upstream, and fished by raising the rod point slowly as the fly comes into the main current, appears to be particularly attractive to the fish.

Such swirling pools are generally deep, and the fish usually take best at and below the point where the heavy boil ends and where the violent surging water begins to grow shallow and to run fanwise, swift and glassy to all sides. There it is well to make two kinds of casts at each stand, one thrown well across to take fish lying in the eddy or on the farther edge of the heavy water, the other barely clearing the heavy water to hang well over fish lying on the nearer edge of the heavy water. Cast thus, the fly will not be swept over these fish as quickly as it will in the former cast when once the swirling current catches it.

On the other hand, when the water is dead low and the fish shy, you will often find that the quicker the fly can be made to sweep over them the better is your chance of a rise.

The soft falling of the fly on the water is not so important when waters are high or coloured, but is a vital matter in low and gin clear streams. People will tell you that it is of no practical importance to cast a salmon fly lightly and without any splash. Pay no attention to them. When the water gets low and clear, light casting—and light tackle too—becomes of cardinal importance. I have, hundreds of times, in low water seen fish bolt off the shallows into deep water when a clumsy cast, of my own or of some other's making, has fallen near them.

Mending (see fig. 21). By this ingenious method you can regulate the speed and action of the fly as it comes round and take the downstream belly out of the line. The Mend is not a cast but a lift

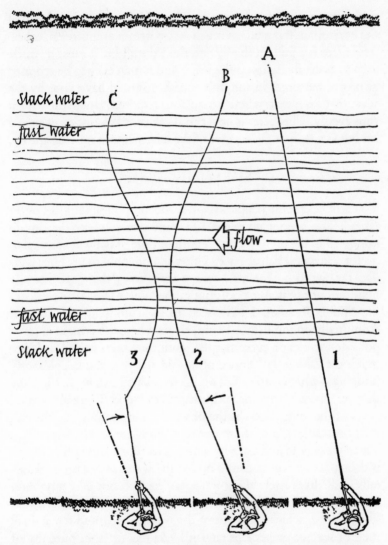

slack water · C

fast water

⟨flow

fast water

slack water

21. "Mending". (1) Cast to A. (2) When fly reaches B the line is taken by fast water into a "belly". (3) By "folding over" or "rolling" the line over without moving the fly you "mend" the line. This may have to be done several times as the fly comes round.

with arms extended and the rod held not high and not much out of the horizontal. It is made as much across stream as upstream, otherwise there is a pull on the fly and this mustn't be. It must be made as soon as the fly lights on the water and it may have to be repeated two or three times in the fly's course. I should have said, by the way, that cases exist where no mend is required, where the stream runs evenly. The secret is never to think of it as a cast or even as a lift but as a Roll or *folding over* of the line, without moving the fly.

"SHEWING" FISH

You will hear some people say—"A shewing (jumping) fish never takes". This is utter nonsense. On some rivers, where the fish do not dwell in the pools for any length of time, it is always as well to go for a shewing fish at once. This will not apply to prolific rivers like the Scottish Dee etc., where sometimes there are literally hundreds of fish in one pool; but in the Welsh Dee, at any rate on the Middle Reaches, I have seen many a jumping fish caught. Admittedly on some (mostly big) rivers where fish remain in some pools for weeks or even months, until they become red, it is not much use taking any notice of an old red fish that is constantly jumping—which some of them do to such an extent that in time they are known by name and usually a *rude* one. There are several ways of shewing. There is the obvious taking RISE when the fish only breaks the top of the water on coming up to *take* something. There is the head and tail rise, which is usually a taking fish. There is the RUNNER which comes out of the water very fast, horizontally, and dives back like a porpoise; he will not take anything. There is the fresh fish, which you can easily tell by its lovely silvery shine, which leaps out of the water, perhaps to try and rid itself of sea lice or perhaps (and it looks like it) from pure joy of life; this fish is always worth trying. Then there is the old red fish who has been up some time; it is not worth taking much notice of him, though of course they do take sometimes. Anyway it is always encouraging to see fish, it always raises one's hopes and when perhaps you have not caught a fish for some days, it does one's morale good to see them.

HOW TO HOLD THE ROD WHEN FISHING

The friendly scoffer thinks that all fishing is a gentle and restful method of enjoying the fresh air and the beauties of nature, and that as a manly exercise it is a mere nothing, perhaps only a little more vigorous than billiards. Tell him that salmon fishing is hard labour and he cannot believe that you are serious. It looks so easy. But if you can only decoy him into a pair of long waders, and put him in a strong water and with a big rod in his hands to attempt a day's salmon fishing you will hear no more criticism of that kind. It is not only that the casting is hard work and finds out all the untrained muscles in your back, but the *common way of holding a salmon rod* when the cast is over is very tiring also. After the cast and when the fly is fishing, the butt of the rod is usually placed against the hip or flank of the angler, and its weight is supported by one hand or the other, which holds the rod some eighteen inches beyond the reel. But owing to the leverage of the long, heavy rod the position is a strained one, and even to strong arms, not hardened by incessant fishing, becomes, in time, very tiring (see fig. 4, 2, page 13).

Before a long day is over your forearm and elbow can literally ache with stiffness in this position, added to the exertion of much casting and you long for some change, to rest the muscles on which the strain falls. Well, there is another and a much easier way of holding the rod either as a change from or as a substitute for the more common mode. The method is this; as you make the cast, one hand, of course, is below the reel and the other is holding the rod about 18in. above it—about the top of the cork handle. As the cast ends, you retain the grasp of this upper hand only, and you draw back the rod until the reel passes your side, placing your right hand on the rod just below the place where the lowest ring usually stands (see fig. 4). You will find that the rod is almost, though not quite, *balanced in your hand*, and further, that you can feel the pull of the line much better, and that you can tighten with greater quickness, yet without excessive force. My own firm belief is that from the time when I learned to hold the rod in this way I have hooked a much greater proportion of the fish which have touched my fly, and have hardly lost any by hard striking. Of course there is no mystery about this way of holding the rod: it is known to many old fishers. Many young ones are inclined to regard it as not quite so attractive as the commoner way. This method is recommended not only for its ease and comfort, but as a great help to quick and certain hooking of fish. I think that the mere drawing back of the rod involved is valuable because in so doing the line is tightened after every cast, but the greatest advantage is the speed with which you get in touch with your fish.

Holding the rod in this way is not difficult to learn, but you can bungle it. Some men never can keep the reel away from their bodies or clothing, or they manage to hold the line so that it cannot go free when a fish takes, but a little practice will solve this problem. It will be found too, that the most comfortable position with a heavy rod is the one where the right elbow is placed upon the rod above the reel (see fig. 4), and the upward pressure of the butt is checked against the right forearm. Even a very heavy rod held in this way seems altogether lighter and livelier.

One hint or two upon carrying your rod whilst walking from place to place on the bank, and especially through woods or bushes. The top seems to flip about much less if the rod is carried almost horizontal and with the *reel uppermost*, and whilst going through trees it is advisable to carry it butt foremost. Furthermore, particularly at dusk, where there is a possibility of tripping and falling, it is essential to carry it butt foremost to prevent damage. If carried over your shoulder, which I do not recommend, you will find that the closer you hold your hand to the point where the rod is resting on your shoulder, the less the rod will flip about behind you. These things may seem trifles to tell you, but when you are carrying a heavy load of fish it is intensely annoying to have your rod constantly slashing against or catching in the trees as you pass them, and it is anything but easy to prevent it.

[4]

How to Fish

There are few subjects in sport upon which more theories are held, about which more nonsense is talked. These theories are held almost as articles of faith and are stated with angry conviction. The truth is that there are many ways to fish well, and no one way is best in all cases. You may fish either deep or on the surface, with flies large or small, plain or gaudy, working the fly or bringing the rod round steadily, and in general you may do well with each method.

The fact that different styles of fishing do hold their ground amongst good fishers suggests—as I believe is the case—that no one style should be adhered to slavishly, and that to fish with the greatest effect one should adapt the methods of fishing to the varying waters fished. And not only do salmon pools differ greatly in character, but the same pool often requires fishing in a totally different place and manner according to whether the river is high or low. One way is to hold the rod almost level over the water and to fish a long line, letting the fly sink deep, and fishing without the least lifting motion of the rod point. The opposite method is with rod held high, as in trouting with a wet fly, and with a rather short line, casting lightly upon the water, keeping the fly always skimming near the surface with a constant lifting motion intended to give the fly a lifelike play. In the rough stream of a medium-sized river, or in deep, strong waters in cold weather, you should fish with a long line cast well down-stream, and allow it to come round as deep in the water as possible without leading with the rod, which is held with the tip only two or three feet above the water. But in low water and warmer weather, and in quiet streams or glassy swirling pools, unless very strong indeed, the fly is cast much more across the stream and worked round by a series of short lifts until the rod is almost upright.

One more caution to you. Be most careful not to bring the rod point round faster than the line is being carried by the current. This is a very common fault but it is a bad fault, for it keeps the line slack instead of taut to the fly. Rather do the opposite and keep the point of your rod *well out over* the stream, particularly if the fly has to swing close in below you. When fishing from the inside of a curving stream you should be most careful to do this.

I would not have any one think that any of these methods are advocated as being necessarily the best, still less as the only good ways of fishing. The more you can vary your fishing with the water the better you will fish.

When you have risen a fish and failed to hook him, you may be in doubt as to what is the best thing to do. If he has been pricked he may come again, but he is not likely to do so. But the mere fact that you have had a hard "pull" does not always prevent the fish taking the fly again. He may not be pricked. I have taken a fish at the fourth offer which had taken my fly hard three times within as many minutes. Sometimes they will take the fly again when cast to them instantly, but some people advise a long wait. Personally I almost always remain where I am, pull in three or four yards of line and from the same stand cast down to the fish by letting out at each cast about a yard of the line drawn in. If that fails, I go out of the stream and begin twenty yards higher up and fish down to him again.

When wading it is a good maxim to take two strides after each cast except when fishing a *known taking place*, or where you have actually seen a fish where you can profitably spend a much longer time. Never take a step forward as soon as you have cast; if you do so the line cannot be doing its job—this will cause a belly on the line and in slack water will drown the fly. A drowned fly is one which sinks lifelessly downwards in the water and looks far from alluring.

Try to feel what your line is doing and to be conscious all the time of the way your fly is swimming in the water. This is the

"Fishing" touch. One important point is that when you start fishing a pool, don't strip off 15yds of line and then start fishing. You could easily have missed a fish lying 5yds from you. Always start with a very short line and lengthen gradually, and furthermore never wade out into a pool further than is necessary (at any rate to start with). You may scare a fish which could easily be lying below you.

In fast running spate rivers, some people fish at any height of water with a dropper—probably a No. 7 double-hook Hairy Mary and a larger single hook on the tail fly, the dropper being about 3ft 6in. from the rod line. Wade into the neck of the pool and throw your line to the side of the stream—about 4yds and "dribble" the dropper just "touching" the water and allowing the dropper to "dance" across the stream. Fish come at it like a snapping dog almost at your feet. Keep on letting out a foot at a time and when the dropper has got too far down the stream for you to make it "dance" any more, then come out and fish the pool down again in the ordinary way.

STRIKING THE FISH

One school of fishers holds that you must *never strike* when salmon fishing and that the salmon hooks himself. Another, that you should always strike from the reel, as they express it; that is to say leaving the line loose and free to run off the reel as you strike. Others hold that you should always strike a salmon just as you would strike in trout fishing, although not so quickly.

These differences, like so many other of our disagreements, exist to a large extent upon confusion of terms. The disputants are often referring to different methods of fishing, and they mean *different things* by the word *strike*. The man who fishes deep with his rod almost horizontal, and so with the point low, will rarely see the fish rise. His first knowledge of the fish is the pull on the line, and if he has had the skill to keep a good taut line, nothing more will be needed to drive his hook home than simply to raise the rod point, or point the rod in towards his own bank and tighten.

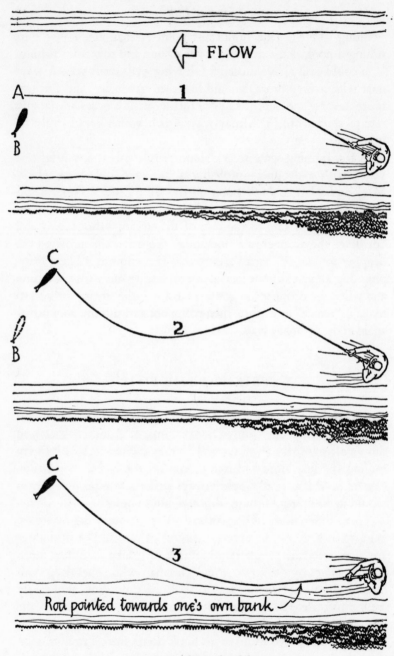

22. Hooking the fish.

In fact it might almost be better to forget the word STRIKE and only talk of HOOKING the fish.

Having cast across the river and mended all the way across (see fig. 22), the fly has arrived at A as in (1). The fish at B has seen the fly and comes up to take it—its impetus carries it on to C (2). The correct action in this case is to point the rod towards your own bank (3). He is then hooked in the SCISSORS on the right side of the mouth, which is the proper and really the only place to hook a fish.

See page 62 *re* trial with hook in dead fishes mouth.

By the prompt, firm raising or pointing of the rod point in towards his own bank (as in 3) the fisher has struck sufficiently; he has driven the hook home into the scissors of the fish, and he needs no sharp stroke like that given by the trout fisher with his quick turn of the wrist. But on the few occasions when the novice does actually see the great boil of the rising salmon, he will generally strike instinctively and—as I have both seen and done—will very often strike too soon.

The man, on the other hand, who fishes with rod point raised and fly near the surface as in trouting (a very good way, too, in clear water), will constantly see the rise; see the salmon like a great trout boiling up at his fly, and indeed he will often see the wave caused by the fish coming to or following his fly. In order to drive the hook home when fishing thus, with rod-tip raised, a sharper, quicker stroke is needed owing to the strain falling upon the thin and yielding top of the rod. But the novice will very quickly find that if he strikes the moment that he sees the boil, he will often fail to hook the fish or even to feel any touch at all. If, however, he waits until the fish has begun to *go down* again, he will very rarely fail to drive the hook in firmly. He should wait perhaps two seconds (see note on double hooks etc. page 19). The best idea that I can give you of the time is this. You see the boil and then you count quietly, one—two—tighten. The fish appears to be then about 2ft below the surface, as you can often judge by the cast appearing above the water. You will very rarely fail to hook him if he has taken the fly.

When fishing with large hooks or with double hooks (see note

on double-hooks page 19) it is advisable, unless the fly has been
taken savagely with a violent pull, to make sure that a marked and
heavy pressure is imparted as soon as possible after you have felt
the fish. This is in order to ensure driving the hooks home. A few
trials with a fly placed in the mouth of a dead salmon freshly
caught will soon convince you that a good deal of force is required
to drive a large hook into the firmer parts of the jaw, i.e. front,
top and bottom, even if *the cast be held near the fly*. Still more so if
about *25yds of line is let out* and the effect of the pull made with the
rod is tested upon the dead fish's mouth. It will be found that often
the barb has not been buried in the fish. Had he been alive and
thrashing about with open mouth, he very probably would have
twisted out the point and would have escaped, as often happens
when brought to the gaff or net when hooked like this.

Fish, in their effort to get rid of the fly in their mouths, do—as
one would expect—struggle and twist about with mouth wide
open. I have myself seen this several times when a bright sun is
shining into clear water below a high bank and has enabled the
early struggles of the hooked fish to be seen with great clarity.

In experimenting with a dead fish one curious thing will be
noticed. The fly, if hooked into the tongue—the very thing which
one would expect the downward-hanging hook to pierce—will
rather easily tear out, splitting the tongue as it does so. No doubt
it is for this reason that one so rarely lands a fish hooked in the
tongue. This splitting of the tongue probably explains some of
those vexatious losses of fish apparently well hooked, which never-
theless escape after a few violent struggles.

Another thing that you must remember is this: never use a
blunt hook. Always keep in your pocket or in your fly case a small
slip of hard whetstone or carborundum to sharpen the point of
your hooks as keen as it is possible to have them. The skin within
the salmon's mouth is smooth and slippery, and the hook should
have a needle point. Here I would repeat that there is only one
sure place to hook a fish and that is in the SCISSORS—if hooked
anywhere else in the mouth, especially in the front, top or bottom,
the hook has to penetrate gristle which is very hard. You should
so hold the line that as soon as the HOOKING is over, or even

before, if the fish should give a sudden savage snatch, the line may be taken freely off the reel. And that is done by holding the forefinger of the upper hand over the line in the following way. You grasp the rod firmly "as in casting", leaving the line quite free. Then detach the forefinger and hook it over the line, closing it again beside the other fingers holding the rod, so that now the line goes under the forefinger and over the three others. Then on a sudden or heavy pull the line will easily and instinctively be allowed to lift the forefinger and thus permit the reel to run. Never under any circumstances have the line twisted round a finger—unless you want it broken. It is much easier to hook a fish taking on the other side of the river. He turns back to his station and this action and the stream ensure that he will be hooked in the *scissors*. It is the fish taking immediately below you which presents a problem.

PLAYING A SALMON

Hold the rod up—this, above all other things, is what you must always remember to do. By this I don't mean that you should hold the rod up perpendicularly all the time because this will not exert enough pressure on him. You will learn only by experience how far down you can point the rod at the fish. It is a dangerous performance and usually implies that you are in a hurry to land your fish. You should never be in a hurry when fishing. An angle of 45° to 60° is a good guide according to where your fish is. In this way you are putting far more pressure on him and will tire him sooner.

But when you really come down to brass tacks two facts stick out:

(1) If your fish is well hooked in the right place you won't lose him.

(2) If you feel that he is lightly hooked, for instance in the tongue (hopeless) or in the upper or lower jaw which consist of hard gristle and teeth then he will probably escape unless you keep firm pressure on him all the time.

So as a matter of principle act on the belief that he is well hooked and try to get him to the net or gaff as soon as possible. From the moment after the fish is hooked until the moment he is gaffed you should never, unless the fish is in the act of leaping out of the water, cease to hold the rod well up.

Next, watch the fish most carefully—If you see him leap out of the water, drop your point instantly, and raise it as soon as he has fallen into the water again. If you feel a sudden quick rush look out for a leap to follow it (see fig. 23) and drop the point of the rod.

Never let the fish rest: when the fish is rushing about and fighting hard, put little strain on it, but keep the line taut (he is tiring himself out), and keep as near as possible to your fish. Always, too, keep the line reeled up so as to have as little line dragging in the water as possible. When he makes a violent and prolonged rush let him go and let him take out as much line as he needs. If a fish makes a normal run there is no point in pulling line off the reel by hand. Let him pull it off himself. It is helping to tire him. The only occasion when you must pull line off the reel and give him all you can is when he has made a prolonged rush downstream and has already taken out much of the backing and the situation is such that you cannot follow him. Then your job is to try and get a belly in the line below the fish hoping that he will think he is being pulled from below. He will often turn upstream towards you. This nearly always works. But the *very moment* he slackens his efforts, *pull him* and *worry him* and in a very short time he will be yours. When the tired fish attempts a run you may easily turn him by putting the rod down-stream and holding it low, and thus pulling his head from the down-stream side, when he will almost always circle round and come nearer to the fisherman and will very soon lose his courage. By this particular manoeuvre you can bring in a slow, sluggish fish in very quick time. Always try if possible to keep opposite or slightly below your fish. Then, keeping a side pressure, you will tend to drown him. As I have said, you should do everything you can to keep near the fish and to prevent him having a very long line out if it can be helped. But at the same time you must take care not to have him on a very short line until he is ready to come to the gaff. If he is within anything like a rod's length of the top ring, he is too close. If he is swimming deep, this does not matter so much, but to have a fish reeled up close that is splashing and struggling near the surface is to invite disaster. Similarly, when the fish is tired and you have to reel him up short in order to use the gaff or net, never hold his head out of the water. Never let the rod point be directly above the fish as if to lift him out of the water, but keep it either down-stream or up-stream of the fish, so that the pull of cast is not a lifting pull. If the fish is being lifted and begins to kick and splash, as he will do—to jigger, as it is called—the jerking on the line is very sudden, and constantly snaps either the cast, the hook or else breaks the hold of the hook.

Casts that we fish with these days are made of nylon and are much stronger than gut—you will soon begin to know when a fish is lightly hooked and requires gentle handling. This matter of being lightly hooked or not is a tricky one. I am told by some of my experienced friends that you cannot possibly tell if a fish is well hooked or not. But I maintain that if a fish is hooked in the scissors (see fig. 22) you can sense that the hold is secure. Whereas if the point of the hook is merely lodged in the front (top or bottom) of the mouth where it cannot penetrate then the feel is different and things become very difficult. The only way you will land this fish is to keep permanent strong pressure on him, except, of course, when he jumps and will probably get rid of the hook in any event. I have often known the hook to fall out of his mouth as soon as he is in the net or on the gaff because the pressure has been released and the hook, having no real hold, drops out. If well hooked and you are fishing with 15 B/s nylon you can give him the butt all the time and never let him rest. A useful tip with a big fish is to PUMP him. This is done by pulling him in a few yards, raising the point without reeling in, then drop the point and reel in without putting much pressure on him until the rod is in position to PUMP him again. Another thing you can do with an obstinate fish is to WALK him—instead of reeling in, you merely walk him up or down the river or if he is stuck on the far side, you walk away from the river; it is quite amazing how he will usually come quite meekly—it would appear that it is the ratchet on the reel which excites him to action—anyway it is a fact that this method seldom fails to move him.

THE LEAP

23. All wrong—the rod should be dropped.

I have often thought of getting a reel made with no ratchet on the reel *in* but only on the reel *out*—like a Silex spinning reel. In this way you can reel in without disturbing the fish. There may be such reels but I have never come across them. A SULKING fish can often be moved by a SHARP TAP on the BUTT of the rod.

An interesting fact which many people do not realise is that if you hold the rod upright, you simply cannot put more than a few pounds pressure on a fish—try it sometime by attaching the hook to some scales and see how much they will register at full pressure—it will only be about 4lb maximum. This may surprise you, it has surprised many experienced fishermen.

TIME TAKEN TO LAND A FISH

With regard to the time taken to land a fish, the old saying is:— 1 minute per lb i.e. 20 minutes for 20lb—don't take any notice of this and further, completely disregard longer times taken. If the fish is well hooked and given no rest he should, in ordinary circumstances and if not a very big fish, come to the gaff in 8–10 minutes or even in a shorter time. The time always seems longer than it is and this largely accounts for people thinking they have had the fish on for ages. As to having a fish on for several hours (unless the fish is foul-hooked), the fisherman ought to be ashamed of himself—he has either let the fish rest or he has got the wind-up that it will get off, which it is much more likely to do the longer he has it on.

In the days of gut casts it was different. Nowadays with NYLON, provided the fish is well hooked and the *knots have been properly tied*, you can, as stated above, give him the BUTT all the time and it is surprising how soon you will have him in; on the other hand if you are faint-hearted and allow the fish to take control it may take a long time to land him.*

* *Editorial note:* I cannot allow these strictures to pass without comment. While I must concede that my first salmon (13½lb on a trout rod) took precisely 3 hours to kill because of fear and inexperience, I have lost in Norway one fish of about 30lb and another in the 55–60lb class after exerting maximum pressure with very

WHEN AND WHERE TO EXPECT SALMON

Cold winds and wretched weather, which send the trout fisher home empty-handed, seem often to make little or no difference to the salmon. The wind and the weather do affect success in salmon fishing, but in a very uncertain and capricious manner. No day and no weather is hopeless if there are salmon in the pools, but a fresh and even a strong wind is usually a good omen for the salmon fisher. Even bitter north and east winds do not prevent the fish from taking the fly, though they can make the fisher pretty miserable, and especially if on his water they happen to be foul winds, that is to say, winds blowing up-stream or in his face. But salmon seem to dislike haze and mist and they seldom take well either in hot and hazy weather or in dull gloom. But if the air is clear and without mist the day may be as hot or as cold, as sunny or as dark as you will, and still you may have a very fine day's salmon fishing.

In big, dark waters a bright sun is a positive advantage, as the fish seem to see the fly better in sunlight, or at any rate they take it much better. But in low, clear water most anglers prefer to have little or no sunshine, although if the day is fresh and the horizon clear and bright a sunny day often proves a very good day and especially in the spring. After a hot, glaring day in August or September the hour of sunset and twilight is never without hope and may prove most deadly. The best chance lasts but a short time and comes after sunset, when the light has failed so much that the surface of the water seems to reflect it all, and you seem to be casting into a river of liquid metal. On such days you should keep one

---

powerful tackle, and both firmly hooked. In one instance, the hooks of my spinner tore out part of the scissors gristle after a downstream pursuit of nearly half a mile. In the other, the combination of sheer weight and my pressure on the fish had the effect of distorting two of the treble hooks so that they failed to maintain a secure hold and came away after about 20 minutes. It is therefore possible to exert too much pressure on a fish but I do admit that many young anglers, through fear of loss and inexperience, tend to treat a hooked fish with undue gentility. But I do not think that this was the case when a member of the Flyfishers Club once played and killed a River Awe fish of 42lb after a struggle of 13 hours.

of your likeliest spots for the last few casts in the failing light, and should be careful to disturb the fish there as little as possible during the afternoon.

Rain is by no means against success in salmon fishing. Rather the contrary, and fish often take well in rain or even in a hail storm. But in very late autumn, when fish are anxious to press on and ascend the river, rain and even showery weather seem to suggest floods and the fish often become unsettled and take very badly in what seems to be almost perfect water. And often at other times when they appear to be expecting a flood, salmon take very badly, although the moment that the water begins to rise they may take savagely. On a quick, sudden rise of water it is well known that fish will take, but it is often said that they will not take in water that is rising slowly and steadily. This may be true in some rivers but is not so in all, and I have often known fish take very well in such water. Even in snowstorms and thunderstorms, and just before thunderstorms, I have known them to rise well, although far more often they refuse to rise at all.

The very worst days are—at all times of the year—warm, muggy days, when the air feels close and heavy and the river is covered with floating foam and bubbles. This foam is a very odd thing. On some days every stream and pool may be covered with flecks and lumps of foam, and every backwater and every eddy is covered with a blanket of hissing bubbles. Such days are more common in autumn than in spring and are always close and muggy days, and the almost soap-sud foam seems to be due to some peculiar state of air and water which delays the bursting of the bubbles formed in the splashing streams. If the day freshens the foam may disappear in a few minutes, but whilst this foam is on the water I have always, or almost always, found the fish take very badly.

As to the places in which you may look for fish, there is no guide like experience and constant knowledge of the water. Even when you have fished a stretch of water for years you may find some place where in certain states of the water salmon take eagerly, and yet you may never before have thought of fishing there.

In high water after a flood. The quiet glides at the tails of long pools, and the thin, glassy water where the tail of any pool sucks down to a rapid below, are usually the most likely places. Also any narrower waist or stronger running place in pools which are, at ordinary level, long, still pools. These places are very deadly in early spring or late autumn, and you may find them by watching the surface of the river when a flood is rising or falling, and seeing where the stream runs strongest and boils most.

In dead low waters. Try the very neck of the stream just where the water running into the pool becomes deep enough to hold a salmon—two or three feet deep—and fish down the rush so long as it is strong enough to swirl the fly about. Also try the strongest swirls of pot holes and broken water.

In bright sun. Fish the streams and in the very quickest part of the streams with small bright and especially with glittering silver or gold-bodied flies. When the sun is very bright, it is never much use fishing a pool when it is shining from upstream straight down the river. Remember the fish are lying with their heads upstream looking straight into the sun. It is better to wait quite a long time until a cloud passes over the sun than to fish the best part of a pool or over a fish you have seen in a good lie whilst conditions are unfavourable.

In wild, rough, windy weather in low water. Fish anywhere, but especially on the quieter flats where lately there has not been current enough to attract fish.

On a rise in the water. Go at once to fish all the places where lately it was too low to fish.

TIDES

(1) Salmon generally enter a river with the INCOMING tide.

(2) It is worth finding out when the tides (especially high or spring tides) come in at your river mouth. The tides are usually published in the local paper.

(3) It is useful to know when to expect a run of fresh fish.

(4) In a Badminton Diary you will find the whole thing worked out for you.

TEMPERATURE

Fishing is best when the air is warmer than the water. The height of the river is important—this can only be learnt locally—and if there is a gauge on your beat, then never pass it without reading it. It will often surprise you to learn that the river has risen or fallen when you did not realise it (see page 36).

So in brief: We see that the best time to fish is after a spate when the river has cleared and is gradually falling and the fish that came up in the spate are settling in the pools. A very good time is 10–15 minutes before a rise. This is sometimes deadly but it is very brief and hard to detect.

An excellent chance is when the river has cleared and is falling after a spate and the fish have not yet settled and you see a fish show at the tail end of the pool, on coming in. Go for him at once, he will not stay there long. But he is almost sure to take you (see page 76).

BAIT FISHING

I am not going to deal with bait fishing at any length for the very good reason that if ever you are going to become a good fisherman I am quite sure that you should learn to fish with the fly first. Bait fishing is by no means to be despised, as it is by the purists (i.e. those who never fish with anything but fly), but there is a definite danger that if you start by fishing bait before you have mastered the fly, you may very likely continue to fish bait, at the expense of the fly, because it is easier and requires much less skill and because it is only human nature to take the easy way. In short —the method of working the bait is much the same as the fly without so many variations and it is much easier to cast—one can learn to cast a bait adequately in a few hours; a good deal depends on the reel, of which there are many different kinds: fixed spool and revolving, etc. The most important thing about bait fishing is the SPEED AND DEPTH at which you work the bait and the size and colour of the bait, according to the water. Speaking generally, wooden baits are the best, you can fish them deep or otherwise, according to how much lead you use. As regards leads, the best sort are those called WYE leads. If you have to add lead, then a Jardine lead is very useful as it can be superimposed on the line without untying and knotting. When using a Jardine it is wise to bend it a bit and this will stop it revolving and causing kinking. If you find your line very kinked, then take the bait and lead off and let the line run free in a strong stream for several minutes and all the kinks will come out.

The rage in some rivers in Scotland is to fish without any leads at all. Some have a very little lead actually inside the bait, being fine lead wire wrapped round the mounting. But in order to fish this style, you should use a fixed spool reel. Some revolving reels will not throw a bait properly without any lead. Fixed spools are much in use these days and when you have got used to manipulating the brakes you will find you can put as much pressure on the fish, as with the thumb on the spool of a revolving reel, but this will take a lot of practice. Of course if you do not master this technique, you will take a terrible long time to play and land a fish on a fixed spool reel. As regards rods, any rod will do the job, but the rod should be stiff and if fishing from high banks it is advisable to have a rod of about 9 to 10ft. You can buy a very serviceable glass fibre 7ft spinning rod for approximately £10 and it is quite adequate. I am not trying to say that any novice can catch salmon with bait—the expert with bait will always catch more than the novice, but the sensible thing to do is to become efficient with fly before starting with bait—so we devote ourselves to learning to fish with the fly first.

Bait fishing is suitable to gentlemen advanced in life and those who only occasionally get a day's fishing. Fly fishing with a big salmon rod can be exceedingly hard work, whereas spinning, especially with these modern fixed spool reels and small 7ft rods is far less fatiguing. An expert can cast the bait exactly where he chooses and double the distance he can throw a fly. When the thermometer is low, it is always worth fishing down with the bait *after* the fly. When the weather becomes milder the spinning rod should give way to the fly. It is said that bait fishing disturbs the pool and that fish will not take a fly after it, but this is a complete fallacy—many fish have been caught on the fly after fishing the pool down with a bait, in fact sometimes it wakes them up. I am not saying that if a prawn is dragged down a pool I would choose that pool to fish the fly immediately afterwards.

FLY FISHING FROM A BOAT

There are various ways of fishing from a boat but the most satisfactory, if the river is suitable, i.e. broad and a good bottom, is to have a 40yd rope and an anchor. By manoeuvring the rope either in the sharp end or slightly down each side you can easily cover a very wide stretch of water, without moving the anchor. The disadvantage in this form of fishing is that, if you hook a fish with the rope fully extended, you will have to pull up 40yds before you can up anchor and pull into the bank. This must always be done because there is a danger of the fish going under the boat and getting foul of the rope. This means that if the fish makes a rush down stream you may need a good deal of backing on your reel. It is always advisable to abandon the anchor rather than attempt to get out of the boat while still at anchor, even if it is shallow enough to do so. By having corks on the end of the rope you can chuck it overboard and pick it up later on.

In some of the big rivers in Scotland and Norway they use a method called HARLING. This to my mind is a very dull form of fishing. You are rowed back and forth across the river, no casting, the rod (or rods in some cases) merely hang out over the stern of the boat and you only wake up when a fish takes. As a matter of interest I would record that my old ghillie J. Parry of Pentre on the Welsh Dee (a man who has forgotten more about salmon fishing than I shall ever learn and from whom I learned a great deal that appears in these pages), tells me they used to fish from a coracle. This must have been an exciting, if not to say, a dangerous job. If you have never seen a coracle, it is oval in shape, 3ft wide by 4ft long, a small wooden keel from head to stern, a few ribs of wood placed across the keel and a ring of pliable wood around the lip (or gunwale). The whole is covered with rough hide, propelled by paddle and only room for one, easily carried on one's shoulders. Imagine hooking a big fish from one of these things, playing him with one hand and paddling for the shore with the other! This was certainly the HARD way—not like HARLING and certainly not dull.

Rowing the boat up river by oar can be very tedious and exhausting. All you need, if the bank is suitable, is about 30–40yds of thin nylon rope, 1,000lb B/s, by attaching it to the cleat about 1yd down from the bows. You can walk along the bank and pull the boat quite easily; someone in the boat must regulate the position of rope in the boat but if correctly placed it will travel parallel to the bank (fig. 24).

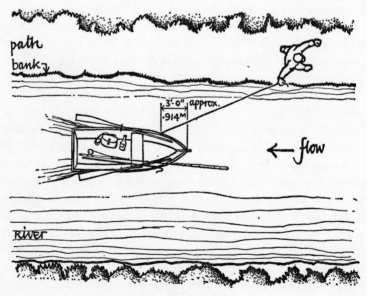

24. Pulling the boat.

WEATHER

Never fail to turn up on the river bank however foul the weather conditions may seem. Except, of course, during and immediately after a big spate, before the river has cleared, when obviously it is hopeless. There are not enough fishing days in the ordinary man's life to risk losing one—even a blank day can be quite enjoyable and instructive if you keep your eyes open. Besides there are always things to be done down by the river, pulling out snags, clearing the banks to improve casting etc. Don't expect to find things all done for you these days, as they were in the days of Water Bailiffs, keepers and ghillies galore.

GHILLIES

I have been very lucky and fished with some wonderful ghillies, not only fine fishermen who were prepared to part with their knowledge, but great characters and wonderful companions. But I regret to say, there are or used to be some of the other sort. Never be upset by their comments and attitude—some of them are very ignorant but it will never do to upset them if you are a stranger on the water and need their advice as to where to fish. Always listen to them—never argue—you may learn something! but never let them tie your flies on or gaff your fish. You have already heard my views about gaffing your own fish (see page 25).

[5]
Catching a Fish

We are now going to go through all the motions of catching a fish. I have chosen a day in April when the conditions are really good— it is a Tuesday and the nets at the mouth of the river were off over the weekend and it was a FULL MOON on Sunday. As we are only 40 miles from the sea, with any luck there should be some fresh fish up. The river is slowly dropping after a nice rise. It has cleared and is at a good height on the gauge—the temperature of the water and the air is good—wind west and slight and some cloud—in fact ideal conditions. We are going to fish a very good pool. We will put on a Hairy Mary, a very good fly on this river (or on any other for that matter) size No. 1/0 or 1½in., which should be about right for these conditions at this time of the year.

We start fishing at the top of the pool and before long we see a fish show at the tail end of the pool at B, obviously a fish that has just come into the pool and has had quite a struggle to get up the rapids. They often break surface for oxygen after expending a lot of energy. Now this is a marvellous chance—proceed at once— don't delay, he will not dwell there long. Take up a position at A and cast beyond where he shewed as (1), so that the fly will come round about 10ft below where he shewed at B. Fish always lie below the point at which they show. Your fly comes round (as in 2)—the fish takes it, his impetus carries him forward as in (3). By pointing the rod in towards your own bank as instructed see fig. 22, page 60, he will be hooked in the scissors on the right side of the mouth. Now, as he has only just come into the pool and you have hooked him right at the tail end of the pool, you must guard against him trying to go downstream again—this would be fatal—

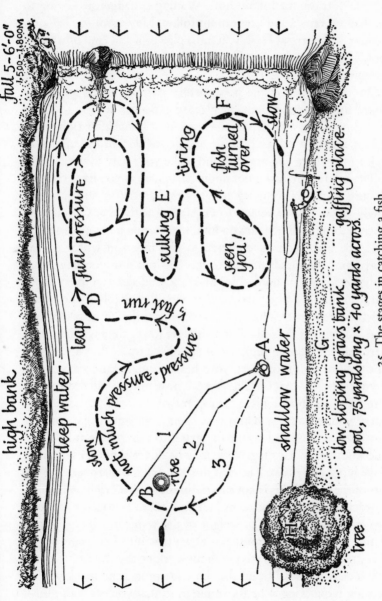

high bank

fall 5'–6'·0"
1.500–1.800M

deep water

not much pressure · pressure.

slow

½ fast run

leap D full pressure

sulking E

tiring F

seen you!

fish turned over

slow

B rise

1

2

3

A

shallow water

G low sloping grass bank.
pool, 75 yards long × 40 yards across.

C gaffing place.

H

tree

25. The stages in catching a fish.

because you cannot follow him. Wading is dangerous owing to
the shallow rapids and you cannot follow him down the bank on
account of the tree at H, so you must play him and land him in the
pool. There is no danger of his going upstream out of the pool on
account of the falls above.

On your arrival at the pool, before starting to fish you have
looked for and found a suitable place to gaff a fish at C.

Meanwhile having driven the hook well home after tightening
on him, you now release pressure on him, while you attempt to get
back from where you are at A and make your way to the bank at
G. The fish meanwhile is not unduly alarmed, as you have released
pressure, and he is cruising slowly upstream. You now proceed
slowly to get out *backwards* to G. Having arrived at G you now
proceed to put full pressure on him, meanwhile making your way
to C, the place you have chosen to gaff him and which is well
away from the rapids downstream. This pressure you have now
applied wakes him up and he makes a wild fast run away from
you; this should convey to you that he will probably make a leap,
which he does at D. Here (as instructed, see fig. 23, page 66) you
drop the point of the rod—but do not get too excited when you see
a large silvery salmon jump clean out of the water. It is a wonderful sight but you must keep your head if you mean to have him.
Having survived that hurdle, you can now resume full pressure on
him. He plays about a bit at the top end of the pool—this need not
worry you, because you know he cannot get out at that end. He
now starts sulking and eventually gets into a deep hole at E. There
is no knowing what snags there may be down there, so you must
move him at any cost. The first thing to try is a sharp RAP on the
butt of the rod. If this is not successful then try retiring again to G
in order to put a downstream pull on him, in fact to try and pull
him over backwards. The weight of the water is helping you. If
all this fails then you must try PUMPING him (see page 65) or
WALKING him (see page 65) without working the RATCHET on the
reel. You will usually find that he will come quite meekly. You
are now wondering if he is coming in so that you can gaff him—
but no! When he gets fairly close he sees you and off he goes, but
not so fast this time and there is no more jump in him. After a

26. Rapids.

while you feel him beginning to tire and then you see him turn over at F. Here he shows the *white* of his belly in the water—this shows you that he is nearing the end. It is now time to get the gaff ready and implant it hook upwards (as instructed on page 26) in the soft ground at the place you have previously chosen for gaffing at C.

Bring him in quietly past you, always from right to left no matter which way the water is flowing. Rod in left hand and gaff in the right. Pass the gaff over his back (as instructed page 27) releasing gently the 2-3ft of slack, lift him out of the water. You must now retreat several feet up the river bank before giving him the *coup de grâce* with the Priest which should be handy in your right hand pocket. Remember not to let him off the gaff (or net) until he is dead.

Having killed him and removed the hook, weigh him; in this case he is a fresh run 18lb fish with sea lice on him—not bad for a first effort! and can you imagine anything giving you a greater thrill—I can't. All this seems to have taken an age but in point of fact, because you have given him full pressure all the time, it has only taken you about 15 minutes—(refer — page 67 "Time taken to land a fish"). Having disposed of the fish out of the sun in some bracken or in some damp grass, you can resume fishing the top of the pool without any qualms about having disturbed the fish. I always hang him up by the tail in the shade, where possible, it preserves his fresh look. As he was a big fish and you had put maximum strain on him, it is wise to renew the whole cast and not merely retie the knots.

If you had hooked this big fish anywhere except at the tail end of the pool, where he was not likely to remain long, then always make a point of casting in exactly the same place where he took your fly. Big fish invariably travel in pairs and it is quite likely you will catch the mate. I have done this several times—it is not at all a rare occurence.

In Conclusion

Whatever kind of fishing you go in for, remember a fisherman must have certain qualities. If you feel that you have not got these qualities, then do not start—you will not make a success of it.

The chief qualities required are patience, a love of nature to enable you to appreciate the surroundings and the bird life, and keenness, and, of course, plenty of time and complete disregard of the weather. Without these you'll never be a fisherman. You must always be prepared to learn. Don't believe all you hear and read but believe all you see and never stop learning. Salmon fishing is undoubtedly the greatest of all fresh water sports. The size of the fish—the surroundings—a large and swift running river—the tremendous uncertainty—the great moment of actually hooking the fish, this thrill remains undiminished as the years go on. The art of salmon fishing with the fly bears no relation to any other form of fishing (except sea trout). There is no analogy with dry fly fishing for trout.

The most essential points are skill in casting and presenting the fly and knowledge of the river. This latter is most important—and skill in playing and gaffing the fish.

I am not going to apologise for what some readers may think unnecessary details. All I can say is that I only wish that when I started fishing (over 50 years ago) I had known of some of these "do's" and "don'ts". They would have saved me a lot of trouble and anxiety. Also, had I known what to buy, I would have been saved much expense. I do not claim the advice given in this book to be all mine, but I have never found it readily accessible in one volume. That is my reason for writing this book in the hope that it may be of some help to my readers.

The Prize

27. Male salmon, the Tay 1907, 57½ lb, 53¼ in. long, 28½ in. girth.

The Prize

Thither ran the river, with its pools dark deep,
o'er the water-rippled rocks above the lies,
and there I went rejoicing through the rocky valley steep,
with my basket, rod and reel, and box of flies.

Rod rings set all straightly, and the line pulled through,
with a Jock Scott tightly knotted to the cast,
my hazel stave a-probing in the water, steely blue,
thus, I set upon my angling way at last.

Swiftly ran the water to the dark fishy lair,
and 'twas here I started casting—cross and down;
on that morning cold and rare, with pine scent in the air,
and the rocks reflected—dark and peaty brown.

Swirled a rise in deeper water, far below,
then I mended fly and line, in one smooth sweep;
it was taken and I struck—with a motion strong and slow.
And he bore away sedately, to the deep.

Flurrying he leap't, as I turned him near the fall,
and I dropped the tip in fear he'ld break and go.
Deep he clove, all solemn sulking, past the rushing watery wall,
as I brought him to'ards the shingle, cross the flow.

With gaff at ready poised, I stood upon the edge;
he went swerving, as he caught me with his eyes,
so ran, tiring—and turned over by the foam bespattered ledge,
and I drew him in and gaffed him then—my prize.

ALEXANDER PRIMROSE

Index